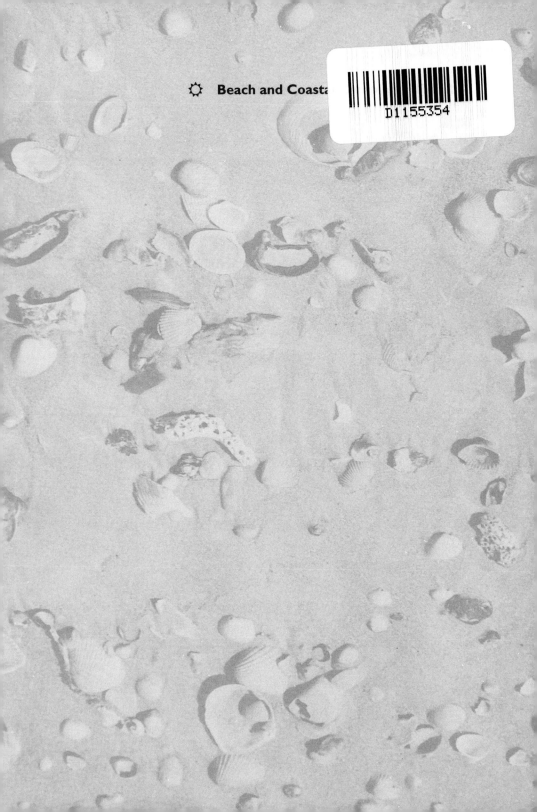

☼ **Beach and Coasta**

Other Books by Johnny Molloy

Day and Overnight Hikes in the Great Smoky Mountains National Park

Trial by Trail: Backpacking in the Smoky Mountains

The Best in Tent Camping: Smoky Mountains

The Best in Tent Camping: Florida

Day and Overnight Hikes in Shenandoah National Park

The Best in Tent Camping: Colorado

Beach and
Coastal Camping in

Florida

Johnny Molloy

University Press of Florida   Gainesville · Tallahassee · Tampa · Boca Raton · Pensacola · Orlando · Miami · Jacksonville

Copyright 1999 by the Board of Regents of the State of Florida
Printed in the United States of America on acid-free paper
All rights reserved

04 03 02 01 00 99 6 5 4 3 2 1

Title page calligraphy by Ken Williams

Library of Congress Cataloging-in-Publication Data
Molloy, Johnny, 1961-
Beach and coastal camping in Florida / Johnny Molloy.
p. cm.
ISBN 0-8130-1682-7 (pbk.: alk. paper)
1. Camping—Florida—Guidebooks. 2. Camp sites, facilities, etc.—
Florida—Guidebooks. 3. Florida—Guidebooks. I. Title.
GV191.42.F6M647 1999
796.54'09759—dc21 98-53597

The University Press of Florida is the scholarly publishing agency
for the State University System of Florida, comprising Florida
A & M University, Florida Atlantic University, Florida International University, Florida State University, University of Central
Florida, University of Florida, University of North Florida, University of South Florida, and University of West Florida.

University Press of Florida
15 Northwest 15th Street
Gainesville, FL 32611
http://www.upf.com

This book is for my old friend and
fellow loyal Volunteer, Tom Lauria

Contents

Preface

There's something special about camping right on the beach—the smell of salt air, the waves lapping you to sleep in your lounge chair, hiking through a maritime forest, canoeing a rich estuary. When someone yells, "Let's go beach camping!" everyone within earshot wants to come along. But where do you go? Well, if you live in Florida or are one of the millions who travel here every year, you have a lot of choices.

That's because the Sunshine State is nearly surrounded by ocean and has 1,350 miles of beachfront, the most in the continental United States. Fortunately for native Floridians and visitors alike, a good deal of this beach and coastline has been set aside for public use. A significant portion of this set-aside land is county, state, or national park property, offering a wide array of scenic and rewarding camping experiences. If you're up to it, you can opt for an ultra-rustic backcountry adventure where you carry everything you need on your back. If you want to be more comfortable, try visiting one of the many recreational facilities in Florida capable of accommodating cars and even those huge RVs. Or try something in between.

In Florida the problem isn't too little choice, it's too much! Matching the perfect campground—and they all have different rules, regulations, and fees—to the needs of your family or group can be difficult if not overwhelming.

And that's why this guide to beach and coastal camping in Florida will come in handy, no matter if you have a pup tent, a van, a pop-up camper and pickup truck, or a souped-up RV. I have found twenty-four of the best places to camp on the beach in Florida, and in this book I give you all the details you'll need to decide which of the twenty-four is for you. They are all great, and in spite of my best efforts you'll still have trouble deciding!

All twenty-four of the campgrounds I discuss here are on public lands. Each individual description opens with an overview describing the attractions of the campground and what to expect. Then comes a description of what the actual beach and coast is like. Following that is a detailed summary of the features and amenities of the campground. I'll also tell you what times of year are best to visit each place.

A section called Key Information will give you explicit directions to the campground and also pertinent data such as phone numbers, fees, the number of campsites available, regulations, reservation availability, and more.

Then, in each case there follows a section called Human and Natural History, which tells a story about the area, perhaps about unusual flora or fauna, or sometimes about the effects of human interaction on the environment. Sometimes the stories are historical in nature, about an interesting figure or special event connected to a place. Some campgrounds and surrounding areas still show evidence of the native peoples who once lived there.

Then comes a section called What To Do, which gives you some ideas on how to spend your precious free time. I tell you where to go to find the best beach walks, historic tours, biking trails, scenic drives, and other natural adventures. If you're into more watery pursuits, you'll appreciate the information on the best swimming, ocean harvesting, snorkeling, canoeing, diving, and pleasure-boating you'll find anywhere.

Finally, a section called What's Nearby gives you the information you need concerning the indoor and outdoor attractions that lie beyond the park boundaries—historic homes, shopping, other parks, and more mainstream tourist attractions. It will also tell you about the restaurants in the area, from four-star to funky.

Now for a word of advice. Before you embark on your camping excursion, learn as much as you can about your destination. If anything in this book is unclear to you or if you have specific questions about issues not covered here, call the park before you leave home! That way you'll have no unpleasant surprises. If reservations are recommended, by all means make them. Of course, there is a certain appeal to striking out on a whim, and we all do it at times. But being turned away because the campground is full can turn a pleasant outing into fodder for a travel comedy movie. Our limited time won't allow for such mistakes.

So, read up, set aside some of your valuable time, pack your gear, and strike out on the open road. The beaches and coastlines of Florida are waiting for you!

Acknowledgments

One of the most rewarding aspects of writing an outdoor guidebook is having the chance to meet many interesting people while you are doing the research. Florida has one of the finest park systems in the country, and its personnel match the scenery. So many of Florida's park rangers tolerated my persistent questions that it's impossible to name them, but I thank them all, especially the strongman at Long Key, the blonde and the redhead at Bahia Honda, Diana at Fort Clinch, and Cecil at St. Andrews. Cecil was definitely the funniest.

I also gathered information from fellow campers. It's nice but somewhat sad how campers cross paths in campgrounds, become friends, exchange stories, and then never meet again. More than a few new friends fed me along the way.

Finally, I would like to thank all my friends back home who made this book a reality, including Hunt Cochrane, Bill Armstrong, Keith Stinnett, Debbie Lauria, Brian Babb, Kevin Thomas, Dean Matthews, Kiki McDonald, and, of course, Meredith Morris-Babb at the University Press of Florida. Happy camping!

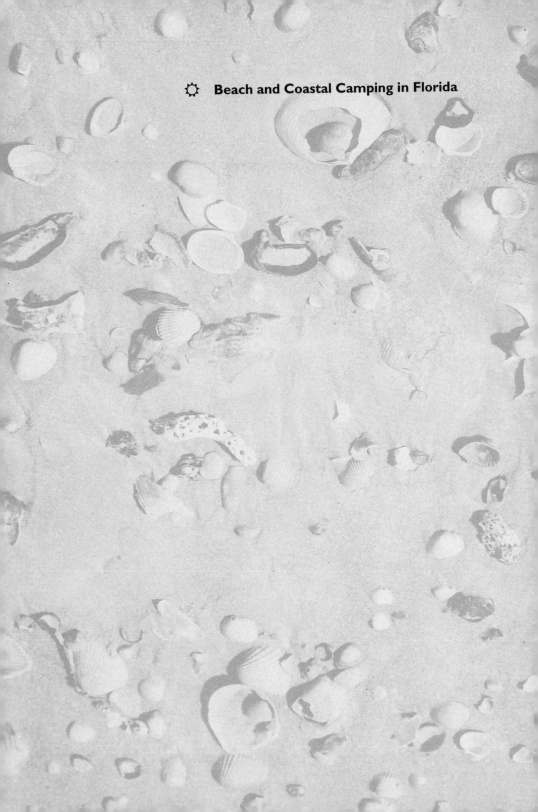

☼ **Beach and Coastal Camping in Florida**

Introduction

The seashore—where land meets water—is a fragile place. Great sand dunes are held in place by sea oats. Living coral reefs grow imperceptibly from the ocean floor. Sea grasses help cleanse the ocean. Estuaries—the breeding grounds for much of the ocean's life—are dependent on just the right mix of salt and fresh water.

This delicate balance is constantly in flux. Wind and waves are forever altering the shoreline. Years of coral-reef growth are wiped out in a single hurricane. Sand dunes are moved by the winds. Floods reshape estuarine salt marshes.

And there is one more important agent of change for beach ecosystems—humans. Condos and other developments flatten dunes and channelize marshes. Propellers damage reefs and rip up sea grasses. Swimmers and sunbathers dump their trash on the sand and in the water.

That's why our shores are more precious now than ever, and why it is our responsibility to take care of them. I've always felt that if you just go out and see the natural wonders of the Florida coast, if you build an appreciation for the beauty and diversity of our distinctive natural legacy, you'll in turn develop a protective attitude toward the coast and all it preserves and nurtures.

And, in fact, humans have long been a presence on Florida's coastlines, and it is truly unrealistic now to expect everyone just to go away. But if we develop the proper attitudes and educate ourselves, we can take those walks on the beach, paddle in the those grassy marshes, motor among the mangroves, and snorkel around the reefs while doing minimal damage to the ecosystem. Combining any of those activities with camping is a great way for families and friends to develop their appreciation for their environment and for one another in settings no theme park can re-create.

And in Florida you'll find some of the finest beach camping anywhere. From the dunes of the Gulf coast, to the historic sites around St. Augustine, to the surfer-friendly central coast, to the tropical and historic Keys, you'll find lots of similarities but also many subtle differences.

West Florida, more commonly known as the Panhandle, extends from the Alabama state line eastward to Apalachee Bay, southeast of Tallahassee, where the coastline curves southeasterly. This curve is known as the Big Bend. Here, creeks drain Florida's highest land, rushing southward and then slowing into salt marshes that give way to large bays. These bays are rich in life; Apalachicola Bay is literally an underwater seafood market. Beyond many of these bays are barrier islands and peninsulas, where famed sugar-white beaches emerge from the sea and rise to great dunes. The dunes form barriers that protect the more fragile coastline toward the mainland.

This is the most heavily forested part of the state, resulting in cleaner waters to mix into the intertidal zone. Pine woods border bays and sounds and the interiors of barrier islands, but give way to more salt-tolerant plants on the beaches. Here are the "wet" deserts, where porous sands drain quickly and plants with long roots such as sea oats tap deeply for water, and where water-conserving prickly-pear cactus grows.

The climate here is Florida's most temperate, with four distinct seasons. During the long summer highs regularly reach the 90s, and a thunderstorm will come most any afternoon. Warm nights stay up in the 70s. Fall finds cooler nights and warm days with less precipitation than summer. Winter is variable. Highs push 60 degrees. Expect lows in the 40s, though subfreezing temperatures are the norm during cold snaps. There are usually several mild days during each winter month. Precipitation comes in strong continental fronts, with persistent rains followed by sunny, cold days. Snow is very uncommon, though not unheard of. The longer days of spring begin the warm-up process, becoming even hot, but temperatures can vary wildly.

The area of north Florida extends from the Big Bend along the Gulf south to Cedar Key and on the Atlantic from the Georgia state line south to Daytona. The Gulf coast here is remote and un-developed and nearly beachless. Extensive forested tracts of land, primarily owned by paper companies, give way to even more ex-tensive marsh and swamplands. These wetlands, virtually devoid of high dry land, have saved this coast from development. Cedar Key and a very few other small islands lie off the coast.

The Atlantic side of north Florida is very different. Large waves pound the shore. The vast St. Johns River forms a large estuarine system beyond which lie the Sea Islands, barrier islands that have played host to history and extend northward into Georgia and South Carolina. The Sea Islands define north Florida. Long ago they were the home of the Timucuan Indians, and then European explorers established rice and indigo plantations there. Later they were the sites of Florida's first resorts. Beyond the island beaches are enormous live oaks draped in Spanish moss. As the islands slope back down toward the mainland, tidal creeks rise and fall among the marshes. Time and nature move slowly here.

Farther south, the Sea Islands give way to high shoreline, with no barriers between the mainland and the pounding Atlantic. Obstinate Coquina rock holds its ground and rises twenty or more feet from the ocean, forming a bluff. The reddish-tan beaches are more narrow in places like Flagler Beach. Barrier is-lands resume just north of Daytona.

The climate is much like that of west Florida except that pre-cipitation patterns follow the rest of the state's peninsula area. A typical year can be divided into two seasons. The wet season starts in June and lasts through September. Nearly half the annual precipitation falls during this time. The rest of the year is relatively dry, with frontal systems bringing rain followed by clear days. Make an exception for hurricanes, though the yearly chance of hurricane-force winds in Jacksonville occurring is only one in a hundred.

Central Florida extends along the east coast from below Daytona Beach to the latitudes that parallel Lake Okeechobee in southern Martin County. An almost continual line of barrier islands with striplike beaches protect the rich estuaries of the Atlantic, such as the Indian River Lagoon, arguably the country's most diverse estuary. From below Cedar Key down to Port Charlotte, the central Gulf coast transforms from marsh to the immense Tampa Bay. Barrier islands line the coast from Tampa Bay through southern Sarasota County. The Gulf barrier islands are not as continual as the Atlantic side, but a maritime hammock exists where development hasn't taken hold. Beaches are more scarce on this side of the state.

The protected waters of Tampa Bay have attracted humans for a long time. Shipping, industrial, recreational, and residential interests all compete for a stake in Tampa Bay while government agencies try to keep the bay clean.

The central coasts have a desirable winter climate for campers, yet it is not quite tropical. Late fall and early spring weather can be pleasant camping weather indeed. Winter days average near 70 degrees, and nights cool down to the 50s. Freezing temperatures are rare, but strong winter winds can make nights chilly. This is the dry season, which usually lasts through May. As the days lengthen and temperatures rise, the heat and humidity results in afternoon thunderstorms. These storms become a regular feature in June and last through September. Atlantic breezes occasionally make humid summer days more tolerable.

This area is within the so-called "lightning belt," where 45,000-amp bolts head toward the ground from one of the more than ninety days of lightning that strike the Tampa Bay area every year. By the time late fall comes, continental fronts are a welcome relief, as they clear the skies and cool the air.

South Florida encompasses a variety of coastal environments. The high, dry, fast-disappearing pine-scrub forest of the Atlantic descends to narrow estuaries and narrow, highly developed barrier islands down to Miami. The mainland coast then becomes marshy, and what a marsh it is. It is the River of Grass, the Everglades, which slowly flows southward into Florida Bay, threatened by agriculture in the north. The islands that are known collectively as the Keys are ancient coral reefs. Now, ringed in mangrove, they protrude southwesterly into the clear waters of the Gulf and stand as the country's most southerly land. Newer coral reefs lie underwater off the coast of the Keys.

On the Gulf side, Charlotte Harbor forms another important component of the southern coast. Large islands such as Sanibel continue south to the northern Everglades and the famed Ten Thousand Islands. Vast thickets of mangrove form these islands, and between them channels provide a course for freshwater flowing out of the Everglades sawgrass. The mangroves form a confusing maze of islands that peters out above sandy Cape Sable, one of the most beautiful spots in the world.

The climate of south Florida attracts a lot of residents and winter visitors. Winter and the dry season bring warm, clear days and mild nights, though cold fronts punch down occasionally, bringing chilly temperatures. But even then daytime highs reach shirtsleeve level. Rain occasionally comes with the fronts, and storms sometimes drift in from the Gulf. Summer warm-up begins in April, and people start thinking about the three h's—heat, haze, and humidity. Afternoon thunderstorms are common. The

Gulf region does not receive strong or frequent breezes like on the Atlantic side, resulting in some sweltering summer days. But proximity to the ocean helps a little, and air conditioning helps a lot.

The Keys experience the most uniform warmth of the humid tropical climate that encompasses south Florida. Winds blow consistently from the east, usually preventing cold-wave invasions from the north. Key West is the only city in Florida that has never officially recorded a freezing temperature. In summer, ocean breezes keep the Keys cooler than most of the rest of Florida, with temperatures rarely exceeding the low 90s and overnight lows in the low 70s. In south Florida, fall is known as hurricane season. The probability of Key West experiencing hurricane-force winds in a given year is one in eight.

Beach Hazards

Every year the lure of sand, surf, and sea brings many visitors to Florida's beaches, and the vast majority of them go home with nothing more than good memories. There are things to look out for, however. While there's no need to obsess over negative possibilities, a little self-education can help ensure a positive outing.

The warmer times of the year are the most popular beach times. This means hot days—and I mean hot. Drink plenty of nonalcoholic fluids, keep yourself shaded for a reasonable amount of time, and cool off in the water to prevent symptoms that could lead to heat exhaustion. Most important, the sun can do plenty of damage on its own. Occurrences of skin cancer are rising rapidly. By all means, wear a hat and use plenty of sunscreen. Of course, shade and clothing are the most effective sunscreens around. I personally try to keep as much of my body covered as I can tolerate.

Beachcombing is a time-honored coastal pastime. Unfortunately, especially in populated areas, trash sometimes washes up on the beach. Watch for nails on boards, glass, and other foot-puncturing items. Consider wearing sandals, especially after the sun starts to go down.

When it's hot there's nothing like a swim in the ocean. Beaches with lifeguards are ideal, but that is not always possible. Exercise caution when swimming and keep apprised of tide and surf conditions. Showing your friends that you're strong enough to swim in a rip tide isn't worth the risk. Use an approved flotation device if you feel the slightest bit uncomfortable in the water, and always have someone swimming with you. And, please, always keep an eye on your children when you're near the water. It takes just a moment to sweep a child out to sea.

Sharks aren't much of a concern in Florida waters, but there are a few oceanic organisms that can ruin your day. There are many jellyfish that can inflict damage. The most notable is the Portuguese man-of-war, whose tentacles can cause severe burns and blisters even if it is dead on the beach. Sea nettles and up-side-down jellyfish cause rashes and itching. Not all jellyfish are toxic, of course, but stay away from all jellyfish as a rule of thumb.

Don't forget that threats run both ways. All of us who want to enjoy Florida's beautiful coastlines also pose a threat to them. When you interact with coastal environments, tread lightly. Picking sea oats destabilizes the dunes. Driving motorized vehicles in restricted areas tears up the landscape. In your boat, watch your prop and don't motor-dredge up shallow waters. Honor fishing regulations. You know what not to do. Think about what you can do. Be a steward for the land. Together we can make Florida's coastline the bountiful beautiful place that we know it can be and should be in the future.

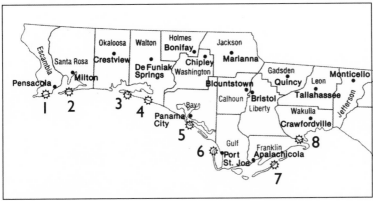

Detail area

1 Big Lagoon State Recreation Area

2 Gulf Islands National Seashore

3 Rocky Bayou State Recreation Area

4 Grayton Beach State Recreation Area

5 St. Andrews State Recreation Area

6 St. Joseph Peninsula State Park

7 St. George Island State Park

8 Ochlockonee River State Park

View of Perdido Key and the Gulf of Mexico from the Big Lagoon State Recreation Area observation tower.

Big Lagoon State Recreation Area

Mix water—both salt and fresh—white sand, military history, and old-fashioned Southern hospitality and you have the Big Lagoon State Recreation Area. Multiple coastal environments overlap at Florida's second-most-westerly state park. Nice folks run Big Lagoon, and their neighbors are good people too. Water is in and all around this refuge, which was purchased and developed by the state in the 1970s. From the beaches along Big Lagoon to freshwater marsh farther inland, recreational opportunities abound.

Key Information

Big Lagoon State Recreation Area
12301 Gulf Beach Highway
Pensacola, FL 32507
(850) 492-1595

Sites: 48 electric, 27 nonelectric

Amenities: Picnic table, fire ring, water spigot

Registration: By phone or at park entrance booth

Facilities: Hot showers, flush toilets, pay phone

Fees: $8 per night November–February, $15 per night March–October, $2 electricity

Directions: From Pensacola, take US 98 west to County Road 293 (Bauer Road). Turn left on 293 and head south to Gulf Beach Highway, dead-ending into Big Lagoon at the end of Bauer Road.

Your entrance fee into Big Lagoon also covers the entrance fee into nearby Perdido Key State Recreation Area, a scenic beach right on the Gulf of Mexico. All manner of watercraft, from speedboats to barges, chug past the park border on the Intracoastal Waterway bordering the park. Overhead occasionally you'll see the Blue Angels and other naval pilots on training missions from the nearby naval base.

There is even some dry land for you to camp on. In fact, the campground is one of Florida's most unusual. It is built on the ridge of an ancient sand dune that offers both vertical and horizontal relief (it has a few hills, unusual for a Florida campground). Big Lagoon is conveniently located to access many nearby Gulf beaches and historical sites. The navy town of Pensacola is just around the corner. It's also one of Florida's most underutilized parks. It's a good place to be and a great jumping-off spot to enjoy the best of northwest Florida.

The Beach/Coast

Big Lagoon has a lot of water frontage offering fantastic views of the nearby barrier islands and sea. The shoreline overlooks the Intracoastal Waterway. On the other side of the waterway are the rolling dunes of Johnson Beach, part of the Gulf Islands National Seashore. Beyond that is the Gulf of Mexico. Big Lagoon has some decent beach of its own. The sand is clean and white, backed by natural pine woods instead of condos. There are two distinct beach areas, both accessible from parking areas by short boardwalks. West Beach juts out into the waterway and has covered picnic pavilions that provide welcome shelter on hot or wet days. East Beach has its own small barrier island and picnic shelters too, in addition to a boardwalk overlooking the salt marsh of Grand Lagoon, where herons and other birds often feed.

The waves are smaller at Big Lagoon than in the Gulf and the water isn't over waist deep for nearly a hundred yards out, making this a safe place for younger and less-experienced swimmers. Just keep one eye peeled for boat traffic and personal watercraft.

Climb the beachside observation tower and look at the maze of land and water below you. It'll give you some understanding of the complex relationship between earth and sea. The towering hotels you can see off in the distance will enhance your appreciation of the $3 million investment the state made to preserve Big Lagoon.

For those who don't want to get sand between their toes, two piers extend a short distance into Big Lagoon. Between the piers is a boat ramp.

The Campground

The campground is actually hilly. Since it was built around an east-west-running sand dune, some campsites are higher than others. Some are cut into the dune and have wooden supports to keep the dune from spilling into the site. Very unusual.

Campsites are located along a long narrow oval. The south side faces a marsh, while the north border is wooded. Overhead is a pine forest with many thickets separating the individual campsites. This thick understory breaks up the site, giving the appearance of solitude, for you can never see more than a few sites other than your own. Many sites are nestled away in little wooded nooks and crannies. But all this vegetation cuts down on the breeze, at times making for a very hot and buggy experience.

The first two-thirds of the camping area has electrical hookups and water, while the back of the campground has water-only campsites. This setup separates tent and RV campers. Most of the electric sites are larger and located on the outside of the loop, so bigger vehicles can get in and out more easily. A dump station is located near the campground entrance. Three fully equipped comfort stations with showers are evenly dispersed in the campground, along with two small playgrounds for little campers.

Park staff recommends spring and fall as the ideal times to visit Big Lagoon. It's not too hot, and bug problems are minimal. It is very quiet during winter. Expect a full house on summer weekends, but campsites should be available during the week.

Human and Natural History

The natural ecosystems at Big Lagoon, especially the wetlands, provide important habitat for birds and land animals such as the fox and raccoon. One critter of special interest is the Perdido Key beach mouse. Listed as an endangered species, this mouse lives only on coastal dune ecosystems, feeding on plant seeds and insects. It cannot change its habitat to a home or garbage site.

The mouse once ranged from Perdido Key all the way up to Pensacola Bay, but development, navigation channels, and intense use by vehicles and pedestrians reduced their habitat. Though it may be only a mouse, it's a strand in the web of life, and when a strand in the web goes, the whole structure is weakened. Plans are to restore a wild population back to Perdido Key. Currently the only wild population is at Gulf State Park in Alabama.

The relationship between the ocean, the rivers, and the land makes the Gulf coast a unique American treasure. And Big Lagoon is really a microcosm of the Gulf. The Gulf of Mexico yields more fin fish, shrimp, and shellfish annually than all of the east coast regions combined. Gulf coast wetlands are half of the American total. Gulf ports handle 45 percent of U.S. import-export shipping tonnage. The Gulf coast provides critical habitat for three-fourths of migratory waterfowl traversing the United States. Ninety percent of American offshore oil and gas production comes from the Gulf. Gulf barrier islands and dunes protect American shoreline. Over twenty billion tourist dollars are spent annually in Gulf coast states.

The future of the Gulf coast will depend on balancing resource cultivation with natural preservation.

What To Do

Within the park confines, there is plenty to do. Beach people swim and sun beside Big Lagoon. Shore fishermen can be seen angling for sea trout, flounder, and bluefish. The shallow waters avail opportunities to go crabbing and cast-netting for mullet. Boaters can use the boat ramp to access the Gulf. Freshwater fishing is done from the bridge over Long Pond, accessible from the Long Pond Trail.

There are several other trails to enjoy. The longest is the "Cookie Trail," which winds from the park entrance to the East Beach and back. It traverses all the different natural environments of Big Lagoon. The Yaupon Trail skirts woods and beach, offering some fine views of Johnson Beach across the water. The Grand Lagoon Trail leads from East Beach through open woods to a shelter overlooking Grand Lagoon. Interpretive exhibits are located along the paths to help you understand the complex environment of Big Lagoon.

Perdido Key State Recreation Area is on the barrier island of the same name just a few miles away. Over a mile of Gulf beach is preserved in its natural state, with wide, white beach and rolling dunes. Shelling can be good in winter. Surf fishing is a year-round activity. Entrance is free if you are staying at Big Lagoon.

Just across from Big Lagoon is Johnson Beach, which is part of the Gulf Islands National Seashore. It is a narrow spit of land with the Gulf on one side and Big Lagoon on the other, with a fantastic beach in between. The beach overlooks the pass into Pensacola Bay. The USS *Massachusetts* is anchored just offshore. There is an entry fee.

What's Nearby

First, get a free map of the locale from the park headquarters. The Pensacola area is rich in military history. The National Museum of Naval Aviation is very near Big Lagoon. It is worth your time, even if you are not a military buff. Admission is free to this converted hangar, where historic planes hang from the ceiling and stand on the floor. In between the planes are interesting displays giving glimpses of life around an airstrip and at war. An Imax theater brings the history to life on a huge screen.

Fort Barrancas is just down the street from the museum. The fort sits strategically on a bluff overlooking Pensacola Bay. When Pensacola was selected for a naval yard, the fort, once in Spanish and British hands, was fortified. The brick fort, complete with a moat and drawbridge, was effective against old wooden ships. Over the years, however, it saw little action, except for a skirmish during the Civil War.

Barrancas had various uses before becoming part of the national seashore in 1971. There is also a picnic area and a short nature trail to enjoy.

Nearby, Advanced Redoubt, another fort, protected Barrancas from land attack. By the time Redoubt was finished, it was obsolete. When you look at Redoubt, realize that poor government planning has been around for a long time.

The Big Lagoon area has plenty of eateries with local flavor. I recommend three. Rusty's is in a wooden building on stilts, with that broken-in, feel-right-at-home atmosphere. Rusty's serves up a mean triggerfish sandwich for a reasonable price. The Original Point has bluegrass pickers and a staff so friendly you think they are just going to sit right down and eat with you. The Florabama is more of a watering hole than a restaurant, but it does serve food. It would be a shame to visit and pass by this stateline tradition.

Just outside the park is a full-service grocery store, and nearby are any other stores you would find in a populated area.

Gulf Islands National Seashore

The Fort Pickens area is the crown jewel of the Gulf Islands National Seashore system. This federally protected seashore covers several coastal areas in Florida and Mississippi. Fort Pickens is located on the western tip of Santa Rosa Island—a seven-mile stretch of preserved barrier island that features a fascinating historic fort.

Once you're past the park entrance booth, a low-lying sliver of white sand sprinkled with sea oats is all that lies before you. Sand spills over the road. To your left, waves crash on the shore, slowly but surely moving more sand. To your right, Pensacola Bay shimmers in the sunlight. After a few miles, trees and dunes appear. The peninsula widens. The campground is off to your right, and boardwalks cross over to Langdon Beach. At the end of the road is

Park ranger leading a tour of Fort Pickens.

☼

Key Information

Gulf Islands National Seashore/Fort Pickens
1801 Gulf Breeze Parkway
Gulf Breeze, FL 32561
(850) 934-2622

Sites: 156 electric, 56 nonelectric

Amenities: Picnic table, fire ring, water spigot

Registration: At campground registration building

Facilities: Hot showers, flush toilets, pay phone

Fees: $15 per night nonelectric, $20 per night electric

Directions: From Pensacola, drive south on State Road 399 for seven miles to Pensacola Beach, passing over a toll bridge. In Pensacola Beach, turn right on Fort Pickens Road and dead-end at Gulf Islands National Seashore.

Fort Pickens, a brick structure that once protected the entrance to Pensacola Bay.

Many lives have passed through the fort, which went through numerous phases from 1829 through 1947, when it was finally deactivated. Today you can walk the beach, ride your bike, and explore the island at will. Other military installations dot this seashore. But it is the miles and miles of pristine beach that will inspire you to return here time and again, to feel the ocean breeze and grasp the beauty of this preserved seaside, while much of the adjacent area is being developed. The campground is spacious, with sites available nearly every day of the year. It makes a good base for exploring other attractions on nearby Santa Rosa Island, on Santa Rosa Sound, and in downtown Pensacola.

The Beach/Coast

Bring your sunglasses to Fort Pickens—the white sand will blind you. Many seaside stretches have little in the way of vegetation. On the Gulf the beach spills over the park border and keeps stretching westward all the way to the tip of the island, where a channel cuts through—the only entrance to Pensacola Bay. As you continue around the perimeter of the narrow island, Pensacola Bay and the naval shipyards come into view. Fort Pickens is just inland, and a few other park service buildings are in the area. The bay side of the seashore has both marsh and beach environments, though minimal wave action keeps the beaches smaller here. The protected coastline continues for seven miles back to the park border.

But go back to the Fort Pickens area. As you look inland, notice a low wall a few hundred yards distant from the fort itself. That was a seawall constructed in 1907 after a devastating hurricane hit the fort. It's pretty far from shore now. Next, look at Fort Pickens. Imagine it being just a hundred yards distant from the ship channel. When it was constructed in 1829, that's how far it was from the shore.

Santa Rosa Island, like all Gulf barrier islands, is migrating westward. Winds primarily come in from the southeast, pounding the shore and pushing the sand. Sand builds on the western ends of the islands while it is being stripped away from the eastern ends. The channel, as well as Perdido Key just across the channel, is also migrating westward.

The Campground

Fort Pickens has a spacious campground, with more than two hundred sites. It is located in the wooded interior of the island. Pines and a few live oaks shade the campsites. Sparse understory vegetation gives an open feel to the campground. The grass beneath the trees is always mown, making it seem like you are camping on a lawn. The bathroom facilities are clean but antiquated. Hot showers are available.

The campground is divided into five different loops. Loop A is located away from the rest of the campground. Electrical hookups and paved parking areas make this the preferred loop for the RV crowd. The other four loops are all connected. Loop B is next to some dunes and has some hills and old military ruins to break it up. Loop C has electrical hookups in an area full of tall pine trees. Loop D has the most spacious sites, including a few under some widespread live oaks. Loop E has electrical hookups also. Some sites look out over Pensacola Bay.

Overall, the campground is clean and well kept, but some of the sites are a little close together. Still, there are plenty of suitable sites. You'll have your pick of the litter during the quiet winter season. Business picks up during spring. Summer weekends are the busiest time, though by evening all campsites may be filled on any summer day. So get your campsite early. Fall is a great time to visit—the weather is good and there are no crowds.

Overnight stays are limited to thirty calendar days per year and no more than fourteen days between March 1 and Labor Day. A dump station is provided for RVs.

Human and Natural History

During the war of 1812 Britain successfully invaded many U.S. harbors, so after the war it was determined that the nation's harbors should be better defended. After the acquisition of Florida from Spain in 1821 (for $5 million—what a deal!), a naval shipyard was built in Pensacola. The construction of Fort Pickens was begun in 1829 and took five years and required the services of hundreds of slaves and a crew from New Orleans. More than twenty million bricks were laid. To hold the massive weight of the bricks and cannons, an ingenious system of arches spread the weight over the packed-sand foundation.

Masonry forts could fire cannons upon wooden ships and expect little threat in return. With the fort in place, no enemy dared attack. That was the idea: to use forts as a deterrent, so they could be manned merely with skeleton crews rather than a large and costly standing army.

The only action at Fort Pickens came during the Civil War, when Confederates occupied nearby Forts McRee and Barrancas. The Union held Pickens, and cannon fire was exchanged. The only casualties occurred when three Union cannon operators were hit by a one-in-a-million cannon shot that came through a small window in Fort Pickens.

In later years the fort went through many alterations. The most visible is Battery Pensacola, located in the center of the fort parade grounds. Built in 1898, it housed cannon. The most famous resident of the fort was the Apache leader Geronimo. When he was in his late sixties he surrendered to the U.S. Army in New Mexico and asked to be reunited with his family. Unbeknownst to him, his family was in St. Augustine, in a crowded Indian holding camp. On the way to St. Augustine it was decided that Geronimo and some of his Apache cohorts should stay at Fort Pickens instead, due to a surreptitious move by local Pensacolans to boost tourism.

So to Pickens he went. And his family was moved from St. Augustine to join him. There he stayed for eighteen months, free to roam the grounds of Pickens. Tourists came by boat to see this legendary warrior. Later he was moved to Alabama, and then to Fort Sill, Oklahoma, where he died.

What To Do

With more than fourteen miles of beach, you can run your toes in the sand and look for shells until your legs drop. By the way, all that sand came from the Appalachian Mountains and is deposited in the Gulf from rivers running from the hills to the flatlands. The sun bleaches the sand white. Boardwalks lead to the most popular beach, Langdon, which is across the road from the campground. Other beach access points are along Fort Pickens Road. You can swim anywhere except in the shipping channel, which is a bad idea anyway. The Blackbird Marsh Nature Trail makes a little loop near the campground, giving you the opportunity to explore another coastal environment. A foot/bicycle trail leads from the campground to the fort. A fishing pier is helpful to anglers, though surf fishing is both popular and productive.

Get a handout and take the driving tour of all the fortified batteries on the island. But the best tour of all is the hour-long, ranger-led tour of the actual fort itself. I loved it. It starts at 2 P.M. daily during the warmer months. A self-guided tour is better than nothing, but the ranger will answer all the questions that will inevitably come up.

What's Nearby

The main attractions nearby are the Naval Live Oaks area of the Gulf Islands National Seashore, the Pensacola Bay Fishing Bridge, and historic downtown Pensacola. Naval Live Oaks is an area that was established by John Quincy Adams as an experimental tree farm to grow live oaks for use in ship building. Now, it is thirteen hundred acres of natural coast on the mainland that harbors many plant and animal communities, including live oaks.

A system of trails runs through the area, including the route of the old Pensacola–St. Augustine Road, which was constructed in

1824. The main national seashore visitor center is here also. There are picnic shelters, an observation deck, and bayside shoreline to explore.

You can drive your car right on the Pensacola Bay fishing bridge, which is old US 98 that crossed the bay. Now you can cast a line from the bridge and catch sea trout, king mackerel, bluefish, and jacks. A convenient fishing camp store is located at the beginning of the bridge.

The Seville Historic District in downtown Pensacola has old museums, churches, and houses you can tour. The historic district visitor center is at the Tivoli House on Bayfront Parkway. The Civil War Soldiers Museum is also located in downtown Pensacola.

Near the Fort Pickens campground there is a camp store with laundry facilities and a pay phone. Outside the park is a convenience store. A full-service grocery store is in the nearby town of Gulf Breeze. Peg Leg Pete's is a good-time oyster bar on Santa Rosa Island. The Sand Dollar Cafe offers all manner of home-cooking with an ocean flavor. Landrys, on the mainland, is a good place for quality seafood.

Rocky Bayou State Recreation Area

Where land and sea meet is often a place of beauty in Florida—anything from white sandy beach to thick stands of mangrove. And the waters are equally attractive and biologically important. In certain instances the state of Florida has recognized the importance of these waters and established aquatic preserves. The waters of Rocky Bayou form one such preserve. The state also saw fit to establish a state recreation area on land abutting Rocky Bayou Aquatic Preserve, making for an appealing place to visit in northwest Florida.

Encompassing an arm of Choctawhatchee Bay just north of the Gulf of Mexico, the aquatic preserve of Rocky Bayou amounts to 480 acres in area, making it the smallest of the state's aquatic preserves. The state recreation area covers 357 acres of mature sand

Shoreline of Rocky Bayou.

pines, a freshwater lake, and an aging but aesthetically appealing
campground that is a meeting place of its own, where campers
can pursue both freshwater and saltwater recreational activities in
the park and environs. Just south of the Choctawhatchee Bay are
the sugar-white beaches of the Emerald Coast, so named for the
color of the ocean waters there. Just north of Rocky Bayou are the
freshwater ponds and clean, clear streams of north Florida's up-
lands, including the vast and accessible tracts of Eglin Air Force
Base.

The Beach/Coast

The state recreation area extends for a mile along the edge of the
aquatic preserve. Much of this shoreline is on a bluff that drops
steeply to an often narrow beach area. In places, wooden stairways
lead down to Rocky Bayou. Pine trees, brush, and grasses grow
right up to the sand of the beach. The translucent waters of Rocky

Bayou, where fresh and salt water mix, are great for swimming. The water is shallow for a good distance into the bayou. These are the calm waters of a back bay, so Rocky Bayou is a safe swimming place no matter what your level of confidence in the water. At the west end of the park near a boat ramp are two small piers that extend over the water. Two little creeks form low-lying areas along the shore. These wetlands may not be visitor-friendly, but they are important habitats that are critical to the aquatic preserve.

If you want waves and ocean scenery the place to be is nearby Henderson Beach State Recreation Area, which stretches more than a mile along the Gulf. The first purchase under the Save Our Coast Program, this scenic beach cost the state of Florida more than $13 million. Pass the shaded picnic shelters and walk the boardwalk to this Gulfside jewel.

The Campground

Rocky Bayou has a small campground situated in a well-wooded area along the bayou and near the park's freshwater locale, Puddin Head Lake. Forty-two campsites are spread along an oval. The eleven sites on the outside of the oval have water only. The other thirty-three, on the inside of the oval, have water and electricity. A concrete-block bathhouse that looks every bit its age has hot showers and flush toilets. The aging facility is clean and well kept.

The campsites are attractively integrated into a diverse forest that is pleasing to the eye. Overhead are many of the mature sand pines the park is known for. Mingled in are live oaks, hollies, magnolias, and turkey oaks—their leaves resemble a turkey's foot. A bushy understory only adds to the shady scene. The individual campsites are large, with reddish-tan sand spread over the camping area floor. RVs can pull in and out with ease. Tenters have plenty of room to set up.

Eight of the campsites look out over Rocky Bayou, though they are not directly waterside. These campsites are the most popular. The campground as a whole gets the most usage during summer, especially on weekends. It is popular with local residents, who bring their tents and oftentimes their boats. This local popularity may have saved the park, which leases its land from the U.S. Forest Service, for at one time there was talk of shutting it down, but locals flooded the capitol with letters of protest and saved it. In the future, look for the state to acquire the land and upgrade the facilities.

Wintertime is slow, with most campers in RVs, on their way farther south. Being a water-oriented park, spring and fall business is dependent on warm weather, but expect to find a campsite during these seasons.

Human and Natural History

Rocky Bayou is one of forty-two aquatic preserves in the state. In 1975, the Florida Aquatic Preserve Act was passed, bringing existing preserves under standardized management. Defined as submerged lands of exceptional beauty and maintained in their natural or existing condition, the aquatic preserves are mostly along the coast, where rich estuaries maintain the delicate balance of salt and fresh water. Rocky Bayou is fed by two creeks and several smaller freshwater streams that mix with the waters of Choctawhatchee Bay.

These preserves are managed in order to maintain the resources that lie within them so that the public can enjoy fishing, boating, and swimming there. Another important mission is to maintain the cultural resources of the preserves. Native middens, which contain Indian remains such as broken pottery and shells, are found at Rocky Bayou.

Another preserve of sorts is located to the north of Rocky Bayou—Eglin Air Force Base. On the base is the largest remaining old-growth longleaf pine ecosystem left in the United States. These pines, two to five hundred years old, are scattered throughout the base, which itself is the largest forest military reserve in the Western Hemisphere. And only 2 percent of the original ninety million acres of longleaf pine woods in the United States are left. So this land is important.

Eglin's Natural Resources Division actively manages the landscape, working with state universities, nonprofit organizations, and industry. Maintenance of the longleaf pine ecosystem is its specialty. More than thirty threatened or endangered plant and animal species benefit from enhancement of the longleaf pine.

Longleaf pines have lost range because of harvesting and replanting with loblolly or slash pine, both of which regenerate faster than longleaf. But Eglin is committed to propagating the longleaf. It is long-lived, more resistant to insects and disease than other pines, and successful on poor or sandy soils. It is heartening to see the longleaf thriving among some of the more than 280,000 acres of the base available for public use.

What To Do

Rocky Bayou is a water-oriented park. Swimming is popular during the warmer months. Many people simply hit the waters right in front of the campground. Others use the many walkways that emanate from the picnic area. Others use the pier area. Rocky Bayou has two exceptional picnic areas separated by a low creek run. The areas are on a bluff overlooking the bayou. Picnic tables are situated among an open wood of pine, red cedar, and magnolia trees. Wooden walkways allow access to the small beach along the bay, where sunbathers can catch some rays.

Boaters will be seen in anything that can be toted on a trailer. Fishermen often use the shrimp in the bay to catch redfish, sea trout, and flounder. Others will either be skiing or pleasure boating.

Landlubbers can enjoy any of the three quality nature trails in the park. Make sure to obtain the handout, which will help you learn about the flora and fauna of the park. Chances are good you will see a deer. The Sand Pine Nature Trail is of special note. It travels along the shores of Puddin Head Lake, a lake impounded by beavers. The lake is fed by what is known as a steephead. A steephead begins where ground water leaks out onto a sloping surface through porous sand. You can try your luck with worms or lures in Puddin Head Lake, where bass and bream swim the waters.

For Gulf waves and ocean scenery the place to be is Henderson Beach State Recreation Area on US 98. Head south of Rocky Bayou on State Road 293, which crosses the Mid Bay Bridge, then west on 98. A mile of beach and two hundred acres of oceanside habitat are awaiting you. In the future, Henderson Beach is slated to have a campground of its own.

What's Nearby

Until I heard about the recreational opportunities at Eglin Air Force Base, it had never occurred to me to have a good time on a military installation. But they have their own Natural Resources Division managing a huge chunk of land just a few miles from Rocky Bayou. To enjoy this land of forests, ponds, and streams, first go to what is known as Jackson Guard. Turn right out of Rocky Bayou on State Road 20 and turn right again in a few miles on State Road 85. Jackson Guard will be on your right a quarter mile down the road. There you can get your map, information, and $5 recreation permit. Or call ahead at (850) 882-4164.

Bicycling, swimming, canoeing, and walking are the most popular activities. Extensive primitive roads make this a mountain bikers' haven. It's easy to get wet in Eglin, with over eight hundred miles of creeks and rivers. Canoeists and fishermen can enjoy the water too. The Yellow and Shoal Rivers are the biggest canoeing streams. But small streams like Titi Creek and Boiling Creek offer intimate encounters with nature. You can even canoe down Rocky Creek and end up at Rocky Bayou. There is a complete map for the canoe trails of Eglin at Jackson Guard.

Bring your rod with you in the canoe or just go to one of the many freshwater ponds on Eglin. These were created, as was Puddin Head Lake, by beavers. Bass and bream are the most commonly sought species.

Many people come to the base to see wildlife such as otter, turkey, and bear. Don't expect to glimpse endangered creatures such as the red-cockaded woodpecker or the gopher tortoise. Some animals are hunted in season. Check to see if the area you intend to visit is being hunted while you are to be there.

Eglin is an underutilized public resource that is waiting to be discovered. Make it part of your Rocky Bayou visit.

Within a few miles of the park are several full-service grocery stores, and there are other shopping and supply places in the nearby town of Niceville. The only restaurants nearby are chain operations, so plan on enjoying a big cookout at your campsite or the picnic area.

Grayton Beach State Recreation Area

A consistent rating as one of the top ten beaches in the United States—including Hawaii—makes Grayton Beach a prime recreation area to visit. Grayton was even rated the number-one beach back in 1994. And it deserves its status as one of the best. Sugar-white sand contrasts with the clear green waters of the Gulf of Mexico. This part of Florida is known as the Emerald Coast. But there's more here than just a sandy shoreline. The beach rises into rolling dunes, splotched with wind-sculpted vegetation that slowly descends into smaller secondary dunes and finally into Western Lake, just on the mainland side of the big dunes.

Dunes of Deer Lake Beach, near Grayton Beach.

☼

Key Information

Grayton Beach State Recreation Area
357 Main Park Road
Santa Rosa Beach, FL 32549
(850) 231-4210

Sites: 36 electric

Amenities: Picnic table, fire ring, water spigot

Registration: By phone or at park entrance booth; reservations accepted eleven months in advance and highly recommended

Facilities: Hot showers, flush toilets, pay phone

Fees: $8 per night October–February, $15 per night March–September, $2 electricity

Directions: From Fort Walton Beach, drive east on US 98 for eighteen miles to County Road 30-A. Head east on 30-A for nine miles. Grayton Beach State Recreation Area will be on your right.

The campground is one of north Florida's best. It has only thirty-six sites cut into an attractive woodland on the shores of Western Lake, close enough to the Gulf to entrance campers with the sound of ocean waves.

But wait, there's more. Grayton Beach State Recreation Area stretches across Highway 30-A with more woodland, which melds into Point Washington State Forest. This forest land allows other recreation opportunities, especially for hikers and bikers. And just a short drive away are three other fantastic beach acquisitions being developed by the state for public use—Camp Helen, Deer Lake, and Topsail Beach. Each beach will make you wonder why you didn't come this way sooner.

The Beach/Coast

The highly rated Grayton Beach extends for a mile along the Gulf. From the parking area a boardwalk extends over the dunes to access the beach. As you walk the boardwalk, look both ways and see how salt spray and wind have shaped live oaks and myrtle oaks into thickets that rise and fall with the undulation of the dunes.

On the water, shorebirds rush in and out with the tide, searching for food. As you walk the beach, notice the whitish haze of sand and spray being forced inland by wind and waves. Great dunes are being constantly altered. Beachcombers access the beach via a boardwalk over the dunes. Another boardwalk leads to the Grayton Beach Nature Trail, which heads inland. The nature trail is very much worth your time, but I wouldn't hike it barefoot.

Western Lake has some decent shoreline of its own. In many places, especially near the campground, the salt marsh gives way to sand, forming a lake beach. Here you can access the clear, brackish waters of the lake. The waves are minimal, and this is a good place to be if the Gulf is too rough.

Camp Helen has a wide beach. Follow the path from the park entrance over a small inlet of Lake Powell, around a dune area to a beach with an old pier. Here the sand extends a good two hundred yards to the dunes. The brackish water of Phillips Inlet splits the beach apart.

Cross an extensive area of dunes to reach Deer Lake Beach. This one is lesser known and more secluded, but only has around a third of a mile of Gulf waterfront. There is a picnic shelter near the parking area.

Topsail Beach has an amazing and costly three miles of Gulf frontage. This area has an extensive dune ecosystem and is still in a wild state. Some of the older dunes are now vegetated beachside hills.

The Campground

Grayton Beach has a well-laid-out, perfect-sized campground. The thirty-six sites are distributed along a classic oval next to Western Lake. What makes the campsite so attractive is the vegetation left in during construction and what has been allowed to grow up after it was laid out in the 1960s. Pine trees are scattered overhead. Sand live oak, yaupon, palmetto, and turkey oak have grown into thickets that form privacy barriers between the campsites. Yet this growth isn't so suffocating that an RV can't pull in and out or tent campers can't spread their gear about.

A fully equipped modern bathhouse is located in the center of the camping loop. Trails have been cut into the vegetation to allow campers to access the bathhouse without cutting through campsites. Short pathways have also been cut from the loop road to access the beach of Western Lake, since only eight of the campsites overlook the lake and have lake beach access paths of their own. Those eight sites are desirable, for not only do they overlook the lake, but also the beach dunes beyond Western Lake.

But the other campsites are no slouches. On the far side of the loop from Western Lake, the campsites are bigger and more open. They back up to a younger pine and turkey oak forest. Campers driving bigger RVs will be more comfortable in these sites. Tenters will want sites closer to the lake to maximize the effect of the breeze.

Each campsite is equipped with water and electricity. Most have live oaks that have been trimmed to shade a picnic table underneath them, because at most sites the noon rays are going to be beating down on much of the area.

The busy season at Grayton Beach starts in March and lasts through the middle of September. Expect a full house every day. Campsite reservations are accepted eleven months in advance and park personnel "most definitely" recommend making them. The publicity of having one of the best beaches in America has its price.

Winter is my favorite time to visit. Campsites are easy to come by. The park is not crowded, and the nature trails and other nearby trails and beaches are a delight to walk.

Human and Natural History

The original 356 acres of the Grayton Beach were leased from the State Board of Education. In 1985, the Save Our Coasts program made five different purchases totaling 812 acres, making for a park total of nearly 1,170 acres. The other three state beach areas nearby were acquired more recently.

Topsail Beach has been declared a state preserve. Formed from ten purchases made over the period from 1991 to 1996, it cost over $100 million. Think about that when you squiggle your toes through the sand. It's a good thing the state bought the property when it did, though, because land values on Florida's coast are only going to rise higher and faster, and eventually every inch of privately owned coastline is going to be developed. These are the facts.

Topsail Beach contains two lakes unique to the entire world. Lake Morris and Lake Campbell, just behind the seaside dunes, are the closest lakes to an ocean without saltwater intrusion. In other words, no freshwater lakes anywhere are closer to the salty sea.

Deer Lake encompasses nearly two thousand acres, but most of the tract is on the mainland side of 30-A. The actual Deer Lake is on the beach side of the road. Yet this tract is nonetheless valuable for preserving oceanside habitat and as a development buffer.

Camp Helen sits high on a hill overlooking Lake Powell and the Gulf. It was first a development that failed and then was an employee retreat for a company from Alabama. It has cabins, cottages, and an old lodge on beautiful grounds grown up with live oaks, hickories, and palm trees. Beyond the lodge is Phillips Inlet and the rather large beach area.

Park staffers say the lodge is haunted by a ghost named Rachel. After the initial development at Camp Helen failed, a man was hired as caretaker. He and his family lived in the lodge. The caretaker's daughter, Rachel, drowned in Lake Powell at the age of eight. Ever since then she has roamed the lodge. Park staffers swear that they hear strange, inexplicable noises. Be advised: Rachel is making them.

What To Do

The highly rated beach at Grayton is the main attraction of this recreation area. Sunbathers and swimmers gather here in the warmer months. Fishermen can enjoy Grayton Beach also. Surf fishing for saltwater species is enjoyed year-round in the Gulf. Western Lake has both freshwater and saltwater species. There is a boat ramp at Western Lake and canoes are available for rental. Park explorers will want to take the Grayton Beach Nature Trail. Here you can safely explore the dunes without harming them. The trail also traverses pine flatwoods, then crosses the dunes on a board-walk and completes a loop via the beach. It's a Grayton Beach sampler. More nature trails are slated for the future.

What's Nearby

With these new acquisitions by the state, Grayton is just one beach to enjoy. If you like a primitive, unspoiled beach, go to Top-sail. Get lost in your thoughts on this quiet stretch of the pan-handle. The two freshwater lakes, Morris and Campbell, offer freshwater fishing. There is a covered picnic shelter near the park-ing area. Future development here will be minimal, as this is a designated state preserve.

To reach Topsail, turn left out of Grayton and follow 30-A to the junction with US 98. Turn left on 98 and follow it for a mile. Look for the entrance to Topsail on your left and follow it to the parking area. Leave your car and the world behind, then let the ocean take your mind away.

My initial sighting of the beach at Deer Lake was memorable. I followed a narrow footpath through dense woods then crossed a small, somewhat high pass between two dunes. The beach opened up before me. Rolling sand, some vegetated, some not, gave way to gentle Gulf water as far as the eye could see. Deer Lake is just a few miles east of Grayton Beach on 30-A.

If you like a little history and a quaint lodge with your beach, visit Camp Helen. The site is undergoing changes, but the walk out to the huge, wide beach and the old rickety pier makes you realize this area has been drawing people for a while. Expect the lodge to be turned into a visitor center.

Hikers and bikers may want to check out the Eastern Lake Trail in the Point Washington State Forest just a few miles away. It has a system of three interlocking double-track loop trails of three, five, and ten miles. These trails wind through sandhills, scrub, cypress ponds, and wet prairie. To get there, turn right out of Grayton, head east on 30-A to the village of Seagrove, and turn left at the second flashing light on County Road 395. Follow 395 for about a mile and look for the marked trailhead on your right.

A trip to yet another state holding, Eden State Gardens, is worth your while. A wealthy owner of a lumber company built a large fine home with well manicured grounds and gardens. His daughter left it to the state. It is located near the town of Port Washington.

The nearest full-service grocery store is in Destin. But Seagrove has a smaller store with most of the necessities. The area also has a few restaurants of note. Located in one building are Picolo Restaurant and the Red Bar. They have been around a long time and have developed the character to match their longevity. The varied menu offers good food for a little money. They also serve up some good live music. The Wheelhouse in Seagrove has the best breakfast, hands down, along with a lunch buffet and inexpensive dinners.

St. Andrews State Recreation Area

St. Andrews is one of the busiest parks in the state. That's because it lies just a short bridge away from Panama City. The 176-site campground is the largest in the state park system. This can create congestion during the warmer months, so be patient and you will find the St. Andrews experience rewarding. But what is the St. Andrews experience? It's an opportunity to camp on a slice of natural Florida surrounded by a thriving tourist town. According to the park staff, generations of repeat campers have been return- ing for this double dose of the Panhandle.

The park wasn't designed this way. When St. Andrews opened in 1951, it was out in the boonies. But the popularity of the Gulf coast beaches and the expansion of nearby military installations resulted in Panama City growing all the way to St. Andrews. So, rather than regarding the park's proximity to the civilized world a

Fisherman on a jetty with Shell Island in the background.

Key Information

St. Andrews State Recreation Area
4607 State Park Lane
Panama City, FL 32408-7323
(850) 233-5140

Sites: 176

Amenities: Picnic table, fire ring, electricity, water spigot

Registration: By phone only

Facilities: Hot showers, flush toilets, pay phone, laundry

Fees: $8 per night October–February, $15 per night March–September, $2 electricity, $2 extra waterfront campsites

Directions: From Panama City, drive west on US 98, cross the bridge over West Bay and continue a short distance to County Road 3031. Turn left on County Road 3031 and follow it four miles to County Road 392. Turn left on County Road 392 and shortly dead-end into St. Andrews State Recreation Area.

bane, think of it as an opportunity to camp in the real Florida while having everything else just a short drive away. "Everything else" ranges from the amusements of the Miracle Strip to fine dining to tacky tourist traps that give Panama City the nickname "Redneck Riviera."

St. Andrews is a worthy destination in its own right. The natural confines of the park contain a nice stretch of beach, clear blue water, high sand dunes, marsh, and a barrier island worth a boat ride. Just remember that camping is by reservation only. Reservations are accepted up to eleven months in advance; you are advised to make them as early as you can.

The Beach/Coast

Civilization can't get any closer to St. Andrews than it is now. The park is surrounded on three sides by water—great news for beach lovers. The sand is sugar white and forms large dunes on the Gulf side of the park. A rock jetty extends into the Gulf and helps keep the channel that is the main entrance to the port of Panama City deep. Sandy Point extends into St. Andrews Bay. The third side of the park stretches along Grand Lagoon, with smaller stretches of sand and calmer waters.

Most swimming and beachcombing takes place on the Gulf side of St. Andrews. No matter how big the crowds, there is plenty of beach for everyone to find a spot. The jetty attracts fishermen. Behind the jetty is a pool of calm water for those who are not willing to tackle the waves coming in from the Gulf.

If you want the experience of walking a deserted, unpopulated beach, go to Shell Island. It is made up of seven hundred acres of protected real Florida stretching for seven miles. Shell Island is located just across the channel from St. Andrews, easily visible from the jetty. The island supports deer and other wildlife, which divide their time between St. Andrews, Shell Island, and the woods of nearby Tyndall Air Force Base. They do this by swimming the short stretches of ocean that separate the three places.

The Campground

Having the largest campground in the state park system and being located near a popular tourist destination presents challenges for the personnel at St. Andrews. It is virtually full from April to October. But they make the most of their space.

Two defined campgrounds lie side by side. All of the campsites are equipped with water and electricity. The Pine Grove Campground has seventy-six sites stretched around three loops. As the name suggests, tall pine trees sway over the camp area. An under-story of palmetto breaks up the campsites. Seventeen campsites face the water. Some feature beachfront and others have sawgrass growing between them and the water. Three older restrooms with showers are in Pine Grove. One of the restrooms also has laundry facilities and a playground for youngsters.

The Lagoon Campground has a hundred sites on either side of Campers Drive. One side of the drive backs up to Grand Lagoon and the other side backs up to a group of ancient sand dunes. Generally speaking the sites here are smaller and closer together. The area also is beneath many pines. Smaller oaks grow here and there, but the farther you go toward the channel the more open the campsites become until there is no cover between sites. Thirty-two campsites are directly waterside.

The Lagoon Campground has two restrooms, two playgrounds, and a dump station for RVs. The bad part is that you can't choose your campsite even in the slow winter season. For the sake of having a year-round uniform policy, you can camp at St. Andrews only by reservation, and you are assigned a site at the office when you pick up your reservation. The sites are given out according to the size of your camping rig and ease of entrance and exit. Park staffers try to keep families and groups together.

If you drive up without a reservation and all the sites aren't re-served, you will get a campsite, but don't even try this during the warmer months. And if you request a waterside site it will cost you two dollars extra no matter what time of year.

Human and Natural History

St. Andrews is on the east tip of a spit between St. Andrew Bay and the Gulf of Mexico. The park proper is five hundred acres in area, with seven hundred acres on Shell Island, just across the channel. But the arrangement was once very different. Once upon a time the spit and Shell Island were one—until the Army Corps of Engineers got involved. In the early days of shipping, it took skillful pilots and a little luck to get into the port of Panama City from the Gulf, traversing a dog-leg turn. Larger ships just couldn't get into the port at all. So in the 1930s the corps decided to make a ship's channel right through the peninsula where the park is today. This made for a straight shot to the port. The corps began dredging and digging on both sides of the peninsula. Train tracks were laid right along the jetty, depositing rocks that would help keep the channel deep and clear.

At some point, a locomotive carrying the rocks fell into the ocean, and it took the corps two years to retrieve the train and finish the job, which dragged on from 1930 to 1938. What they ended up with was a deep, wide channel and Shell Island. So Shell Island is not quite as pristine as folks make it out to be. But it is still beautiful and worth a visit.

The St. Andrews story wouldn't be complete without a telling of the story of Teddy the Hermit. Teddy was the park's beloved first resident. Well, actually he had been living there since 1929. Before he came to St. Andrews he'd been living on his boat in a nearby marina. But in September of 1929 he had his boat dry-docked for repairs. As fate would have it a hurricane struck. Teddy tried to stay with his boat but ended up fleeing inland. Later he returned, only to find his boat, thus his home, missing.

After searching the area, he found the remains of his boat near where Campsite 15 is today. The boat was in bad shape, but Teddy resolved to repair it. Meanwhile, he made a little shack to live in while the repairs were being made. He eventually realized that the boat was beyond repair, and he made his shack, which sat near Campsite 101, more livable. Teddy made a life for himself on the island with his cats and chickens. He hand-dug a well for fresh water. For cash he sold fish to a local market and would come to town every now and then for goods he couldn't get from the wild.

In 1946, the state of Florida acquired the land and gave Teddy, then sixty-four years old, a lifetime lease. Park visitors would come and see him. It is said that he was the main attraction in the park in its early days. Teddy passed away in 1954.

The circular overlook you see near the jetty is actually a cannon platform from the World War II era. The forests of St. Andrews were also turpentined earlier in this century. There is an actual turpentining still located on the island that was moved here from Bristol, Florida.

What To Do

Everybody loves a beautiful beach, and St. Andrews has one. High dunes make for good vantage points. Or you can walk right next to the waves. Summer finds many swimmers and snorkelers, especially around Shell Island. Divers explore wrecks farther out to sea. There is a dive shop right by the jetty.

Fishing is very popular here. Why not, with surf fishing, a Gulf fishing pier, jetty fishing, and a bay fishing pier? Something's always biting. Catches often include redfish, flounder, Spanish mackerel, king mackerel, bluefish, and grouper, all without ever leaving land. If you do want to venture out into the water, canoes and kayaks are available for rent. There is a boat launch if you have your own watercraft.

Or you can take a shuttle to nearby Shell Island. This is a favorite with most visitors to St. Andrews, especially the glass-bottomed boats. The shuttles operate during the warmer months and are fairly inexpensive. Walking the beach on Shell Island is worth the price.

St. Andrews has quality interpretive trails and programs. Make sure to check out the turpentine still and then walk the Heron Pond Pine Flatwoods Trail. It's less than a mile in length yet packs in a good overview of beach ecology. The same goes for the Gator Lake Trail—you learn a lot in a short distance. But if you actually want to see an alligator, go to the Buttonwood Marsh. There is an overlook at the freshwater marsh there where alligators are often spotted.

What's Nearby

Panama City and Panama City Beach are tourist destinations for thousands annually. There you'll find attractions to fit most any taste and budget. Gulf World features a marine show with dolphins, sharks, and other ocean creatures. Six acres of fun are at Shipwreck Island, a water park with rides, slides, and other wet escapades. Miracle Strip Amusement Park offers more than thirty rides that are a little drier than Shipwreck Island. Bettors may want to try their luck at Ebro Greyhound Park, where the dogs race. Bungee jumping, miniature golf, go-cart racing, and more round out the entertainment.

Any number of ocean activities, such as boating, sailing, and riding wave runners, as well as charter fishing, scuba diving, and more are also available.

Captain Anderson's is a classic local eatery just outside the park. They take pride in serving only fresh local seafood, and it's been there for more than thirty years. Canopys offers fine dining. The Black Angus in Panama City is the choice for steak lovers. With the city so close, there's something for everyone.

The park itself has two camp stores with limited supplies, and the store near the jetty has a dive shop. But just across the bridge in Panama City is a city full of stores of all kinds.

St. Joseph Peninsula State Park

A beachside wilderness area containing the highest sand dunes in the state, located right on the Gulf—could this be? Yes. This wilderness preserve, two fine camping loops, white-sand beaches, and more are all part of St. Joseph Peninsula State Park. The crowds aren't too bad either, but if you really want to get away from it all, load your backpack or kayak and camp in the wilderness.

Located about fifty miles southeast of Panama City, St. Joseph is located on a narrow spit of land jutting out into the sea. The Gulf of Mexico is to the west. The waters of St. Joseph Bay lie between the 2,516-acre park and the mainland. Miles of sugar-white

Looking out on St. Joseph Bay from the park wilderness preserve.

Key Information

St. Joseph Peninsula State Park
8899 Cape San Blas Road
Port St. Joe, FL 32456
(850) 227-1327

Sites: 97 electric, 23 nonelectric

Amenities: Picnic table, fire ring, water spigot

Registration: By phone or at park entrance booth

Facilities: Hot showers, flush toilets, pay phone

Fees: $8 per night November–February, $15 per night March–October, $2 electricity

Directions: From Port St. Joe, go east on US 98. Go three miles and turn right on County Road 30 and follow it eight miles. Take the sharp right turn on County Road 30-E and follow it for nine miles. You will dead-end into the park road.

---

beaches line the perimeter of the peninsula, while the interior is forested.

The state has unobtrusively developed St. Joseph. You'll appreciate the amenities—marina, camp store, and bathhouses—knowing that no development is allowed in the wilderness preserve.

The Beach/Coast

There is far more beach than there are people at St. Joe, surrounded on three sides by water. The blinding white beaches are backed with striking sand dunes rolling the length of the peninsula. There are three primary Gulf beach-access areas and two primary bay-access areas. The main beach is across from the marina area, where the peninsula is only a hundred yards wide. Cross the dunes on a boardwalk and the Gulf opens before you. To your left lies the civilized world beyond the borders of the park and to your right are miles of protected beach, where the blue ocean, white sand, and tall dunes meld into the distance.

Each of the two campground loops has access trails leading to the beach from the camping areas. The trail from Camp Area 2 is a little more than a hundred yards in length. The bay access is from the Bay Trail, which leaves from the picnic area. This beach is smaller and narrower. The forest grows nearly to the bay in spots. The bay is shallow and you can wade far from shore, exploring the wildlife-rich body of water. Horseshoe crab skeletons litter the shoreline. This side of St. Joe is quieter and less windy, though the

Dunes along St. Joseph Bay.

view of the mainland tarnishes the "deserted island" effect. The other bay-access area is on the Coastal Hammock Trail, which starts near the park entrance.

The Campground

There are two camping loops at St. Joe and they each offer their own experience. Camping Area 1 is located between a marsh and sand dunes. It is an open, RV-oriented campground with a smattering of pine trees that offer moderate shade. A few palms break up the grassy center of the loop, which holds fifty-nine campsites, all with electrical hookups. The ocean is on the far side of the dunes, so you can clearly hear the waves lapping the shore. A good ocean breeze keeps down the insects. The center of the loop is grassy, with a smattering of palms. Campers have a single bathhouse for their convenience. The outer part of the loop is sandy, with a scattering of brush. Crossroads bisecting the loop allow RV traffic to move safely and freely.

If you like a lot of sun and have an RV, stay in this loop. It is closer to the beach than Camp Area 2. There is little to screen campers from one another, so you might as well make friends with one and all.

Camp Area 2 is deeper into the park, located in the forest interior. Longleaf pine, coastal live oak, and sabal palm shade the fifty-one-site loop, which doesn't benefit from the ocean breeze as much as the other loop. Two fully equipped comfort stations serve the area. Campsite privacy is provided by a dense understory of palmetto and yaupon rising high between the sites. Intermittent grassy areas add to the attractiveness of the campground.

The first half of the loop has electrical hookups and supports tent or pop-up campers but no RVs. The woods are too thick to navigate an RV in this area. The rest of the loop has water-only sites, mostly on the inside of the loop. This is the exclusive domain of tent campers. The sites are defined by dense brush and are a little on the small side, though there are a few larger campsites on the outside of the loop in a low spot that could prove a regrettable choice during a rainstorm. No matter where you camp, store your food properly, as the raccoons here are notorious food bandits.

The campground is busy during the spring break season. Scallopers and families fill the campground during summer. Warm days and cool nights lure some campers here in fall. Winter offers solitude and occasionally mild weather.

Adventurous campers can head to the wilderness preserve for some backcountry camping. You must first get a permit at the camp office. Smart campers will bring their own drinking water. For the sake of endangered sea turtles, no gulfside beach camping is allowed. This is a great getaway, though from experience I don't recommend backpacking the preserve in the heat of summer.

Human and Natural History

St. Joe occupies the end of an L-shaped peninsula that extends first west, then north into the Gulf of Mexico. It protects the mainland from the direct wrath of the sea. Several types of plant communities can be found here. The older interior dunes are covered in sand pine scrub, while pine flatwoods occupy more level areas. Fresh and salt marshes dot the woodland. Sea oats stabilize the huge dunes.

This spit was first occupied by Indians. They reaped the undersea gardens of St. Joseph Bay. Later, the family of T. H. Stone ran cattle on the peninsula. Just prior to the onset of World War II, the Stone family sold its land to the U.S. Army for use as a training facility. The United States still owns the property and leases the land to the state of Florida for use as a state park. Nowadays, an Air Force installation and an ever-increasing number of beach houses occupy the first few miles of the peninsula. Then the state park begins.

Within the state park are huge dunes. During summer months the white beaches harbor a special treasure: turtle eggs. Loggerhead, green, and leatherback sea turtles come ashore during this time and lay their eggs, which incubate between fifty and seventy days. The male turtles spend their entire lives at sea, while females leave the water only to lay eggs. The hatchlings head toward the sea to test long odds against survival to adulthood.

St. Joe is on the flight route for spring and fall bird migration. More than 209 species have been recorded here. Shore and wading birds are year-round residents. There is plenty of life on land as well. White-tailed deer are the critters you'll most likely see. The gray fox, bobcat, and skunk are other components of the web of life in the preserve.

What To Do

St. Joe has plenty to offer active campers and beach enthusiasts. Sunbathers have miles of beaches on which to relax and escape from the daily grind. Shelling is productive on both beaches, but especially on the bay side of the park. Scalloping brings back visitors year after year. The season generally runs from June 10 to the end of August. Check with the park for current rules and regulations. Fishermen can surf-cast for a variety of fish on the Gulf or wade the flats for sea trout in the shallow bay.

Boaters can enjoy the waters no matter what the size of their craft. The park marina offers docking and launch facilities for larger boats. Canoes are for rent, but can only be used in the bay, weather permitting. A canoe or kayak is a great way to explore the preserve. Paddle along the shore of the protected bay, beach your craft, and explore at will. I've enjoyed many St. Joe canoe camping excursions this way.

Birdwatchers will be found throughout the park. The wilderness preserve, covering the last 1,650 acres of the peninsula, can be enjoyed by foot for a day or a weekend. You can enter the wilderness one of three ways: by walking the Gulf beach, the more difficult bay beach, or the seven-mile interior fire road. I've done them all and like walking the fire road best. Other fire roads split off the main fire road and lead to the Gulf or the bay. If you follow the fire road to its end, you will come out on the bay just short of the peninsula point. Follow the beach around to the large sandy point and see both the Gulf and the bay. On your way, check out some of the marshes with cattails growing on their edges. The fire road starts at the end of the cabin road.

What's Nearby

Nearby outdoor attractions include the St. Vincent Island National Wildlife Refuge. St. Vincent Island and nearby Pig Island are accessible only by boat. About forty miles northeast is the vast Apalachicola National Forest. Highlights include a portion of the Florida National Scenic Trail and some great freshwater canoeing streams such as Kennedy Creek and Owl Creek. The national forest is over a half-million acres of trees, trails, and rivers that offer a variety of outdoor experiences.

A camp store at St. Joseph State Park offers minimal food, camping, and fishing supplies. Just outside the park is a small convenience store, Cap'n Jacks. Two other convenience stores are on Cape San Blas. Beyond this, you must travel back to Port St. Joe to find a grocery store or bank. Port St. Joe also has some decent restaurants, but the nearest fine dining is in Panama City.

St. George Island State Park

St. George is one of the largest barrier islands on Florida's Gulf Coast. Until 1965 it was accessible only by boat. In 1963 the state had purchased the east half of the island, sparing it from development. Today we can enjoy nearly two thousand acres of unspoiled barrier island, where beaches, sand dunes, and pine trees guard the Apalachicola Bay, which lies between St. George Island and the mainland.

Upon entering the park, the first thing you'll notice is the blinding white sand. The beach rises from the blue ocean waters. Then, where sea oats can grab a foothold, dunes begin. Further inland, bushes take root, and older dunes rise high above you. Beyond the large dunes lie the pine forests, interspersed with oak

Beach at low tide.

Key Information

St. George Island State Park
HCR Box 62
St. George Island, FL 32328
(850) 927-2111

Sites: 60

Amenities: Picnic table, fire ring, water spigot, electricity

Registration: By phone or at park entrance booth

Facilities: Hot showers, flush toilets, pay phone

Fees: $8 per night September–January, $15 per night February–
August, $2 electricity

Directions: From Apalachicola, drive east on US 98 and cross John
Gorrie Memorial Bridge. Turn right on County Road 300 and cross
St. George Sound to St. George Island. Then turn left on Gulf Beach
Drive and follow it for four miles to the dead-end at St. George Is-
land State Park.

trees. Beyond the forest lies a narrow beach and the rich waters of
Apalachicola Bay. Ponds and grasses dot the island interior, breaking up the woods.

Across the bay is the town of Apalachicola, an old Southern
town where most folks make their living from the sea. Marine
fare culled from the bay is sold on the waterfront. Further inland
are the historic ruins of Fort Gadsden, surrounded by the half-
million acres of the Apalachicola National Forest.

All this is easily accessible from the sun-splashed campground
on St. George. Here you can get away from it all, yet easily get
back to it all to enjoy civilized pleasures and nearby attractions.

The Beach/Coast

There are nine miles of undeveloped beaches to explore within the park. To see how valuable this land is, check the prices of the beach homes leading up to the park. You'll see why—sugar-white sand and rolling dunes with nothing but clear Gulf waters extending as far as the eye can see. It's a short walk from several auto pullovers to the land's edge, where storms scatter shells. There are two designated beach areas with covered picnic areas, restrooms, and outdoor showers. Between the parking area and the beach, a boardwalk traverses the dunes.

The bayside beaches are smaller, with less wind and waves but more solitude and potentially more bugs. Boats are often seen in the bay, and the trees of the mainland form a skyline.

The eastern beaches of the park are very remote. There are three ways to explore them. Hikers can follow the five-mile fire road to the East End, where sand, sea, and sky merge, or beachcomb along the Gulf. Adventurous fishermen in four-wheel-drive vehicles can purchase a special permit at the ranger station and drive to the point.

The Campground

The campground lies four miles from the park entrance, in the interior of the island behind some rather large dunes. But it's not so far that you can't hear the surf crash against the shoreline. The sixty sites are spread along a narrow oval. Set up your tent on the grassy floor and park your vehicle on the crushed oyster shells. Water and electricity are available at every site. There are two fully equipped restrooms with showers spread along the loop.

Most of the campsites extend outward from the loop and are divided by bushes that offer some decent privacy for your campsite. Some sites are more open than others. The first half of the loop has smaller campsites that abut dense vegetation. These are appropriate for tent campers. RV enthusiasts will like the sites on the second half of the loop. There the campsites are larger and more open, with plenty of room to maneuver a house on wheels.

Slash pines are interspersed throughout the campground and offer a little shade. A few smaller oaks offer some shelter from the sun, but around noon the campground gets a whipping from Old Sol. Bring a tarp along with your tent for a refuge from the rays. No matter where you camp, store your food properly—the raccoons are brazen daylight camp robbers and beggars.

From September to February, St. George is pretty quiet, but expect a full campground around Thanksgiving and Christmas. Spring breakers from up north will fill the place up. You can find a spot during weekdays in the summer, but expect a full house on weekends. Reservations can be made up to eleven months in advance.

St. George also has a primitive backcountry campground located on Gap Point overlooking Apalachicola Bay. But it takes a little work to get there. Backpackers can walk the 2.5-mile trail through the island's interior. Boaters can embark from one of the bay ramps and canoe or kayak to the campsite. Remember to register at the ranger station and bring water.

Human and Natural History

St. George is a Gulf barrier island that forms the southern edge of Apalachicola Bay. It is twenty miles long and only a mile wide at its widest point. Formed five thousand years ago, the island was uninhabited until this century. But early in the twentieth century the turpentine industry came to milk the island's slash pines. During World War II, St. George was used for military exercises. The construction of a causeway in 1965 opened the doors for habitation and access to the park, which opened in 1980.

You can still see evidence of turpentining on many park pine trees along the interior island trail. Black vertical barkless areas with V-shaped scars show where, in winter, incisions were made in the trees using galvanized metal gutters. A special kind of clay pot known as a "gerty cup" was put below the gutter. Then, in summer, resin flowed into the gerty cup. The pine resin would be distilled into oil of turpentine, which was used for explosives, detergents, and in shipbuilding.

The beaches and dunes support limited wildlife. Raccoons are the island's biggest residents. Osprey are the lords of the skies. Terns and other shorebirds can be seen. But the bulk of life around here lies beneath the ocean.

As a barrier island, St. George shelters the bay from the powerful ocean. From the mainland flows the large Apalachicola River. It is here, between the river and St. George, where fresh water and salt water mix, forming an estuary. This combination forms a fertile environment and supports a wide variety of plant and animal life. These marine resources are the source of 90 percent of the state's oyster harvest, which is centered in the nearby town of Apalachicola. Shrimp, bluefish, and crab are also part of the reason nearly three of every four townspeople make a living from the sea.

Apalachicola was first settled in the 1600s as a trading post. During the rise of cotton in the Old South, it grew to be an important port city. Nearby Fort Gadsden was ruled under four different flags. Now Apalachicola is surrounded by sea on one side and vast forest lands on the other.

What To Do

Sunbathing and beachcombing are the two most popular activities on St. George. Swimmers dot the ocean in summer. Be advised that there are no lifeguards on the beaches. Hikers have three good trails from which to choose. The fire road leading to the East End extends for five miles, so make sure to bring water. Two other trails lead from the campground. The 2.5-mile trail to the primitive campground winds through the center of the piney interior and ends at Cape Point. The soft tones of the trees and brush give your eyes a break from the blinding white beaches. Another trail leads a little more than a mile to the north side of the island and overlooks the bay. Bicyclists pedal the quiet road along the island.

You can fish in the surf or the bay. Many people use frozen shrimp for flounder and Spanish mackerel. The bay side is said to be productive for redfish and sea trout. Two bayside boat ramps give canoers, kayakers, and motor boaters access to the sea.

What's Nearby

A trip to nearby Apalachicola is mandatory for St. George visitors. The bridge across the bay offers a great view of the area. If you like fresh seafood, as in just off the boat, get some from one of the many oceanside markets. The restored historic district is fun to walk around. Tasteful clothing, gift, and antique shops inhabit the brick buildings along with a few restaurants and galleries.

A good place to eat is the Apalachicola Seafood Grill and Steakhouse. Their specialty is a whopper of a fried fish sandwich—dubbed the largest in the world. Take note that the restaurant's ice is made using John Gorrie's original recipe. Gorrie invented the ice machine, and a museum in his honor is just around the corner. He created the ice machine to cool rooms and prevent malaria. You might call it primitive air conditioning. Risa's Pizza is also in the historic district. There are some small but decent grocery stores in town where you can buy supplies.

Just a little farther inland on State Road 65 is the Fort Gadsden historic site. First built by the Spanish in 1814 along the Apalachicola River, it later fell into British hands until Andrew

Jackson wrestled Florida away from the British and Seminoles. Later, the Confederate Army occupied the fort. This site is surrounded by the half-million-acre Apalachicola National Forest, with a network of trails and rivers extensive enough to keep any outdoor enthusiast busy.

St. George Island has a few convenience stores for quick necessities. Two island eateries of note are Oyster Cove and Island Oasis.

Ochlockonee River State Park

Tucked away in the maze of rivers, sloughs, bays, salt marshes, and estuaries that makes up the Big Bend coast of Florida, Ochlockonee River State Park is figuratively and literally a hidden jewel of the Florida state park system. With two rivers marking park perimeters, this aquatic hideaway allows park visitors to indulge in fresh, brackish, and saltwater pursuits. Camping facilities, trails, and drier habitats are found on the 392 land acres of the park. The park is surrounded by wild lands administered by the Apalachicola National Forest, the St. Joe Paper Company, and the St. Marks National Wildlife Refuge. In fact, Ochlockonee River State Park was culled from leased lands of the wildlife refuge.

Campground shoreline by the brackish waters of the Ochlockonee River.

☼

Key Information

Ochlockonee River State Park
P.O. Box 5
Sopchoppy, FL 32358
(850) 962-2771

Sites: 24 electric, 6 nonelectric

Amenities: Picnic table, fire ring, water spigot

Registration: Ranger will come by and register you

Facilities: Hot showers, flush toilets, pay phone

Fees: $8 per night September–February, $10 per night March–August, $2 electricity

Directions: From Sopchoppy, drive south on us 319 for four miles. Ochlockonee River State Park will be on your left.

Things move slow in Wakulla County. The fast-paced lifestyle of the condo and resort set hasn't reached this part of the coast. Keep that in mind when you amble in and find yourself a site in the small and scenic campground. After you set up, head out and go for that big redfish. Or snooze in your hammock, or visit the wildlife refuge, or read a book, or swim at the dock, or watch the pines grow, or go to Wakulla Springs, or canoe the river, or hike in the national forest, or go to Carrabelle Beach, or . . . you get the picture. Just remember, everything moves at a leisurely pace, Southern style.

The Beach/Coast

The park lies where the Ochlockonee River and Dead River converge, making for a fair stretch of waterfront. Only seven miles from the Gulf, the waters here are mostly brackish, and heavily influenced by the tides. Several oceanside habitats thrive nearby. The park sits on a bluff overlooking the rivers. At one end of the park a boat ramp leads into Tide Creek, which meanders a short distance down to the Ochlockonee River. Quietly, salt water moves into the creek, then moves back out a little less salty than it came in.

The Ochlockonee River is wide here, even with an island in the middle of the waterway facing the park. A trail meanders along the pine-, oak-, and palm-lined river bluff. Where the campground is nearest the river, two wooden platforms lead from the bluff to small beaches along the river. Across the river is a marsh, where moss-draped cypress trees grow tall among the grasses.

An attractive picnic area lies where the Ochlockonee and Dead Rivers meet. Live oaks and hardwoods shade picnic tables, which overlook the waters beyond them. No fewer than five wooden walkways emanate from the picnic area, accessing the shoreline.

Adjacent to the picnic grounds, a sandy beach leads to the park's roped-off swimming area. An L-shaped dock juts out into the Dead River, complementing the swim area. Across the river is a vast sea of rushes and Thom's Island, part of the St. Marks Wildlife Refuge. Beyond the swim area, pine flatwoods grow up to the Dead River's edge beyond the park and into the refuge.

The Campground

I really like this campground. It's small. And smaller is often better when it comes to a campground. This one has only thirty sites. It backs up to the Ochlockonee River. A white-sand road sprinkled with pine needles forms a horseshoe through the campground. Live oaks border and shade the campsites, most of which have grass and sand floors. Clumps of palmetto and other brush break up the area and form campsite barriers for privacy.

As the horseshoe turns, three campsites are set back from the road. These are more secluded, nonelectric sites designed for tenters. Other sites on the inside of the horseshoe are very shady under a near canopy of live oaks. Most of the campsites are situated on the outside of the loop. Three more nonelectric sites are situated away from the road on the second turn of the horseshoe and are the sites closest to the river—close enough for a view of the Ochlockonee, but not directly riverside. The other twenty-four campsites have water and electricity.

The end of the loop has more pine- and oak-covered campsites, some very shady. You can look over the grassy playground for kids. There are three pull-through sites for large RVs, though many other sites are RV-friendly. All campers will like the new bathhouse. It is fully equipped with flush toilets, hot showers, inside and outside sinks, a pay telephone, and a soft-drink machine.

Summer is the busy time here. When school lets out, this campground will fill up. Come early in the day and you should get a site. No reservations are accepted; you must take your chances. You can always camp in the nearby national forest, then take your chances again the next day. Spring and fall are exceptional times to enjoy the park and the nearby wildlife refuge. A few hunters and RVs traveling south are the only wintertime visitors.

Human and Natural History

The Big Bend coast is a mosaic of different habitats that support a diverse collection of flora and fauna as well as shaping human interaction with the land. An exotic but startling park denizen is the albino squirrel. It seems that back in 1969 a man from Illinois set up a hunting camp across the river, bringing a cage full of albino squirrels with him. One night a member of his party had a little too much booze and set the squirrels free. They established a colony at the hunting camp. Then, some either swam across the river or floated over on debris, establishing a second colony here in the park. So don't think you're plastered when you see a white squirrel running up a tree at Ochlockonee River.

The St. Marks Wildlife Refuge protects more Florida-esque landscapes that inhabit the Big Bend coast. The refuge covers nearly sixty thousand acres from the Ochlockonee to the Aucilla River, where alligators, waterfowl, bear, otter, and dolphins call home. It was originally established in 1931 to provide a wintering habitat for migratory birds. It still does.

This was human habitat for pre-Columbian Indians, who prospered in this resource-rich coastline. Spaniards found the area appealing, founding the town of St. Marks and building Fort San Marcos de Apalache, which you can visit today. Another interesting structure is the St. Marks lighthouse. The 1831 beacon is still in use today. Both the lighthouse and fort were sites of Civil War maneuvers.

Until the establishment of the refuge, salt extraction, turpentining, livestock raising, and lumbering provided area residents with a living. St. Marks is just one of more than five hundred federal wildlife refuges nationwide, conserving more than 92 million acres of wild land. The first refuge was established in 1903 on Florida's Pelican Island, where birds were being killed for their feathers. Refuges are established not only as places for migratory waterfowl to stop over, but also to protect wetlands and the endangered species that call these places home.

Within a wildlife refuge, any manner of management tools are used to ensure that the flora and fauna of the region thrive. Areas of public use are shifted to protect animal reproduction, native grasses are planted, other spots are burned over, and forests are thinned. Other areas—designated wildernesses—are left undisturbed. This includes more than 21 million acres of wilderness in the entire wildlife refuge system. While wildlife refuges protect natural resources, they also allow visitors many outdoor recreation opportunities.

What To Do

Ochlockonee River State Park makes a great recreation base, whether you enjoy only the park resources or those beyond its borders. Having two rivers nearby makes swimming and fishing a natural choice. The several small beaches and the designated swimming area can become busy on hot days, with sunbathers using the picnic area as a place to bring their coolers and spread out their towels.

Because there is a boat launch, shore fishing is not the only angling option. Boaters can head out to the Gulf, to explore the maze of rivers and bays of the coastline. Get a map of the Lower Ochlockonee River from the park office before embarking. Skiing is another pastime for boaters. Canoes are available for rental from the park at a very reasonable rate. Tidal creeks and protected estuaries make for rewarding wildlife study areas from a canoe.

If you are fishing, don't be surprised at what ends up on your line. This is one of those habitats where both fresh and saltwater species inhabit the local waters. Bass, bream, speckled trout, redfish, and flounder can be caught.

Bicyclers can pedal park roads, especially the Scenic Drive that meanders through the park's pine flatwoods. Hikers can walk the River Trail or take the informative loop hike that starts near the picnic area.

What's Nearby

The natural world dominates the landscape on the Big Bend coast. Park staffers will help you navigate your way around the area. Nearby state holdings are Wakulla Springs and the San Marcos de Apalache fort. Often claimed as the world's largest spring, Wakulla Springs pours forth water so clear that glass-bottomed tour boats are extremely popular. The surrounding forest is laced with nature trails. Near the fishing village of St. Marks is the San Marcos de Apalache fort. You can tour the grounds and museum and gain an understanding of the area's importance in the settling of the continent.

Nearby federal lands include the St. Marks refuge and the Apalachicola National Forest. The Sopchoppy and upper Ochlockonee rivers, as well as small streams such as Kennedy Creek, offer canoeing through secluded national forests. Hikers can enjoy a portion of the Florida National Scenic Trail, which passes through the Bradwell Bay Wilderness.

You must visit the lighthouse at St. Marks National Wildlife Refuge. It is at the end of Lighthouse Road, which many visitors bicycle. Hiking, canoeing, nature study, fishing, and boating are other ways to enjoy the refuge, which is open from sunrise to sunset.

The nearest Gulf beach is at Carrabelle, about fifteen miles west of the park. Bring as much in the way of supplies as you can to Ochlockonee River State Park and expect to do your own cooking. The nearest full-service grocery store is in Crawfordville, though there is a small store in Sopchoppy, four miles from the state park.

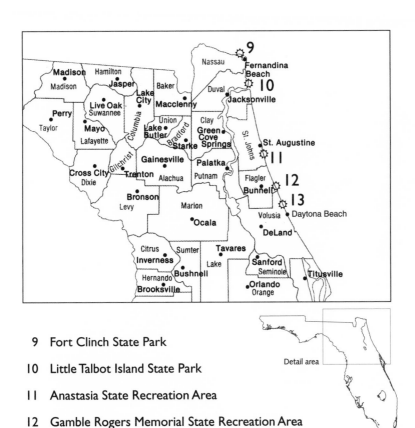

9 Fort Clinch State Park

10 Little Talbot Island State Park

11 Anastasia State Recreation Area

12 Gamble Rogers Memorial State Recreation Area

13 Tomoka State Park

View of Fort Clinch from Cumberland Sound.

Fort Clinch State Park

Why should a beach camper come to Fort Clinch State Park? To see a restored brick fort, to camp in either of two appealing and diverse campgrounds, and to enjoy three types of ocean environment. Fort Clinch is located on the northern tip of Amelia Island, which happens to be the most northeasterly point of the state. Here the Atlantic Ocean gives way to Cumberland Sound and the Amelia River. The state of Georgia is just across Cumberland Sound from Fort Clinch.

History buffs, fishermen, hikers, mountain bikers, and beachgoers can all enjoy this park. Reenactments and candlelight tours are held at the fort, which is open daily. There are several

---

☼

Key Information

Fort Clinch State Park
2601 Atlantic Avenue
Fernandina Beach, FL 32034
(904) 277-7274

Sites: 62

Amenities: Picnic table, fire ring, water spigot, electricity

Registration: By phone or at park entrance booth

Facilities: Hot showers, flush toilets, laundry, pay phone

Fees: $17 per night, $2 electricity

Directions: From the town of Fernandina Beach, drive east on A1A for one mile. Fort Clinch State Park will be on your left.

---

different ways to fish here. The ultra-long park pier is just one way to pursue the big one. Hikers and bikers can enjoy a newly constructed path that winds among old forested sand dunes. And you will find the beach can be just as relaxing as either of the two campgrounds.

The Beach/Coast

Nearly a mile of beachfront looks out over the Atlantic Ocean. The sand is tan and gently sloping. Here sunbathers and swimmers cool off in the waves. A jetty first built during the Spanish-American War in 1898, then rebuilt since then, extends more than a mile into the Atlantic. This makes the sand extend out in a point before turning beyond the jetty. Beside the jetty is the two-thousand-foot pier that ocean lovers and anglers enjoy.

As the shore turns west into Cumberland Sound, dangerous currents prohibit swimming, but beachcombing is welcomed along the one and a half miles of beach that abut the sound. The beach is not as wide here as the Atlantic. Human-placed rocks indicate the beginning of Fort Clinch. At one time beach erosion threatened the north bastion of the fort and the rocks were placed here to prevent the erosion. Across the sound is Cumberland Island in Georgia.

The coast turns back south as you pass a small fishing dock and boat ramp. Here the Amelia River is wider than the sound was. However, the beach has narrowed, and the shoreline slopes sharply. Red cedars and live oaks grow close to the water. The Amelia River narrows, then gives way to Egans Creek, which is a classic sea island tidal creek flowing amid grassy marsh.

Other nearby beaches on Amelia Island are Fernandina Beach, run by the city of Fernandina Beach; American Beach, with its big dunes; and Amelia Island State Recreation Area, where you can rent horses and ride them on the beach.

The Campground

There are two distinctly different campgrounds at Fort Clinch, and campers will tell you they have a strong preference for one or the other. The first campground is the Atlantic Beach Campground. It is located behind a series of dunes near where Cumberland Sound and the Atlantic Ocean meet. It has a simple oval design, with all twenty-one campsites on the outside of the oval. The oval is surrounded by a low wood barrier that prevents campers from tromping in the dunes. There is a boardwalk that leads to the beach.

A few palm trees are the only shade in the campground, and they are in the center of the oval, with the brick bathhouse and laundry. The campsites themselves are sand and grass. The low profile of the vegetation has its advantage—an ocean breeze that minimizes insects. The view of the surrounding sand dunes is nice too. But that ocean breeze in winter will keep you in your RV, for the beach campground is the domain of the big rigs. RV campers seem to bond in the Atlantic Beach Campground.

The other campground is the Amelia River Campground. It is in the shape of an oval cut in half by a sandy road. The campground borders the Amelia River. The campground road is paved until it reaches the boat ramp and then is sandy as it completes its loop. The forty-one campsites are set in a shady coastal hammock forest. Most of the campsites are rather large and have a decent amount of vegetation between them. Just a few of them have a view of the Amelia River; the vegetation is too thick and the surrounding forested dunes are too high everywhere else. Wooden barriers keep the vegetation growing well between the campsites.

Overhead are live oak draped in Spanish moss, an occasional magnolia, and some large red cedar trees. The understory is primarily yaupon, red bay, and palmetto. Two brick comfort stations serve the campground. This campground will be cooler in the summer, the price you pay will be a few extra bugs. Tent campers form the majority here, though RVs will always be seen as well.

Fort Clinch has been growing in popularity; there once was a distinct off-season in the coolest months. Don't be misled—in winter the campground only fills on weekends. But after March it can be full any day of the week. Summer weekends will be full. Business slows somewhat after Labor Day and campsites can be had any day except for nice Saturdays.

Human and Natural History

The modern history of Fort Clinch began in 1842 when the United States purchased the north end of Amelia Island for a military installation that was to be part of a program to protect our country's seaports. This fort would protect the mouth of the St. Marys River, which flows out of Cumberland Sound and the port of Fernandina. Construction began in 1847. The fort was named after General Clinch, who served during the Second Seminole War.

By the beginning of the Civil War, Fort Clinch was only partially completed. That is the reason you see two kinds of bricks in the fort. The first bricks came from Georgia, but after the conflict began no more bricks were coming from there. The top bricks were shipped from New York.

The Confederates were the ones who first took possession of the partially completed fort. But the Union captured several forts up the coast, and Fort Clinch was left isolated, so the Confederates abandoned it.

Construction was renewed after the Yankees took over again but was not completed even after war's end. Then the fort was deactivated until the Spanish-American War in 1898. After that brief period of activity, the fort continued deteriorating. During World War II, however, the Coast Guard used it as a surveillance post. By this time it had passed from the federal government to private hands to the state of Florida. In the state's hands, Fort Clinch became one of Florida's first state parks. During the Great Depression the Civilian Conservation Corps developed much of the park. It has been well taken care of ever since.

What To Do

A tour of the fort is mandatory. See the cannons, the jail, the officers' quarters, and the courtyard. You might be one of the lucky ones to see the fort come alive during a reenactment. These take place during the first weekend of every month and on special occasions. Rangers and volunteers dress in costume and live life as it was during the 1860s, going about their chores. They will be happy to answer your questions about what they are up to, but they know nothing of life after the 1860s. Special candlelight tours are held during summer. But even if you miss one of these events, tour the fort anyway—the views from the top are spectacular!

The beach is a year-round attraction, though sunbathing and swimming are warm-month propositions. Ecotourists are always

Cannons at Fort Clinch.

seen shelling and birdwatching. Walk the beach along the sound and along Amelia River. Fishing can be done on the surf, from the pier, or from a boat put out from the boat launch. Sheepshead and whiting are popular pier catches. In the Amelia River, redfish and sea trout will be caught. Crabbing and cast-netting for mullet are done too.

Bicyclists can tool the main park roads, and mountain bikers have an additional treat in store for them—a six-mile trail that winds among the ancient sand dunes of the island interior. Hikers can also enjoy this trail and the foot-only Willow Pond Nature Trail.

What's Nearby

Just across Cumberland Sound is Cumberland Island National Seashore. It can be reached by boat, canoe, or kayak from Fort Clinch. If you have no watercraft, you can take a ferry to Cumberland Island from St. Marys, Georgia. There are miles of trails in the interior and sixteen miles of beach to explore as well. There are also two old mansions on the island. The ruins of Dungeness are the remains of a plantation built by Nathaniel Greene. Plum Orchard is still standing and is a huge sight to see.

On the south end of Amelia Island is Amelia Island State Recreation Area. This is one of the few places left on the east coast where you can ride horses on the beach. Rides are secured through reservation. Call (904) 261-4878 for reservations.

The town of Fernandina Beach has a restored historic district. There are coffee houses, antique stores, and buildings that hearken back to another time. The Coffee Cafe and Bretts are two recommended eateries in the historic district. Also in the town is a full-service grocery and discount store. There are a couple of convenience stores near the park.

Little Talbot Island State Park

Little Talbot Island is one of the largest undeveloped barrier islands in the state of Florida. Located on the northeastern coast near Jacksonville, Little Talbot is one of the Sea Islands that stretch northward up the coast into Georgia and South Carolina. These islands are characterized by wide sandy beaches along the Atlantic, thick maritime live oak hammocks built on ancient dunes in their centers, and grassy saltwater marshes cut by tidal streams dividing the islands from the mainland.

True to form, Little Talbot is a gem. The beach is one of the most pristine in the country. The wooded center is junglesque in its lushness. The grassy salt marsh is a scenic estuary where much

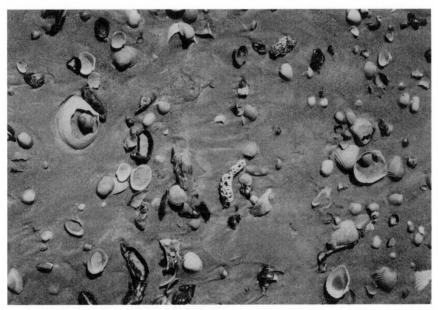

Shells along the beach of Little Talbot Island.

Key Information

Little Talbot Island State Park
12157 Heckshear Drive
Fort George, FL 32226
(904) 251-2320

Sites: 40

Amenities: Picnic table, fire ring, water spigot, electricity

Registration: By phone or at park entrance booth

Facilities: Hot showers, flush toilets, pay phone

Fees: $8 per night October–February, $14 per night March–
September, $2 electricity

Directions: From I-95 in Jacksonville, take State Road 105 north
(Heckshear Drive) for twenty-two miles to Little Talbot Island State
Park, which will be on your right. State Road 105 becomes A1A
after passing the ferry to Mayport a few miles before Little Talbot
Island.

of ocean life begins. Nearby islands such as Fort George and Big
Talbot accentuate the historic and ecological importance of the
Sea Islands. On Fort George, the remains of a cotton plantation
and a military fort show how barrier islands have been used in the
past. And the incredible beauty of "The Bluffs" on Big Talbot Island must be seen to be believed.

The Beach/Coast

Fort George River separates Little Talbot Island from Fort George
Island to the south. The pass between these two islands is a widely
fluctuating tidal flow that covers and exposes sandbars. Along the
Atlantic side of Little Talbot, you first pass the park observation

deck, which was being separated from the island by the shifting nature of barrier islands as this was written.

Then begins five miles of wide beach that gently slopes up from the Atlantic. Due to the strong tides near the Fort George Inlet, swimming is not allowed here. Farther north begins the multiple-use beach area, which is connected to parking areas by five different boardwalks. This strand is backed by sea oat–covered sand dunes that extend all the way to the north point of the island, which reaches Nassau Sound. The big waves by the point are favored by surfers.

As you make your way back south around the island, a grassy salt marsh begins. Simpson Creek is the main watercourse flowing through the grass. A boat launch and small sandy area is located near the park campground, then the marsh continues south to meet the Fort George River.

Just a little north of Little Talbot is Big Talbot Island. A stretch of the island fronts Nassau Sound. Here tall bluffs drop straight off to a small beach littered with skeletons of live oaks that have fallen into the sea. Rock formations break out of the sand at points. You can look toward the salt marsh or over at Little Talbot Island or beyond the shifting sandbars of the sound into the Atlantic. Bring your camera to this beautiful and distinctive beach.

The Campground

Pass the locked gate from A1A and enter the campground via a sandy road that winds behind some ancient sand dunes. These large dunes block much of the wind, especially the strong winds of nor'easters, as I once found. The forty-site campground splits into three two-way roads that each have a little turnaround. Two fully equipped bathhouses are located between the three loops. Campsites range in size, and the park will put you in a site according to the size of your outfit. All the campsites have water and electricity. Shade is generally the rule, although there are some fairly sunny creekside campsites.

The right-hand loop passes by a huge forested dune. On your left are four campsites beneath live oaks covered in ferns. The understory is adequate, primarily yaupon and palmetto, but leaves a little to be desired in the way of campsite privacy. Two campsites are off by themselves on the turnaround, while two others are on their own little spur road. These last two campsites overlook the salt marsh.

The middle loop is more level than the first loop. The main road has campsites under live oak, southern magnolia, and holly, but pines and palm begin as you head toward the salt marsh of Simpson Creek. The campsites on the turnaround are sunnier and have views of the creek. Some of the open campsites have wooden fence barriers as dividers.

The main road of the left-hand loop has several deeply shaded campsites. The campsite floor is sand, but vegetation springs from the ground everywhere else. Things open up a bit as the turnaround passes the boat ramp and comes to three campsites that look directly over the scenic grasses of the marsh. Some of the smallest campsites are in this loop.

Overall, this campground is attractive, and even though some of the campsites are pinched together, the small size makes everyone a little more neighborly. I get a feeling of everyone being in on the secret of having found this great place. It is a good campground on a pristine island that is perfect for nature lovers.

Come March, Little Talbot Island gets busy. Everyone loves to come to the beach in spring. You can count on nearly every weekend being filled. During the week there are usually a few open spots. It's the same way through the summer, but don't be surprised if the campground fills on a weekday. The place clears out in September, even though fall is a great time to visit. In the winter, Little Talbot really slows down. But on the first pretty weekend after a prolonged spell of bad weather, the campground is flooded by locals. Throughout the year, about half of the campers are RVers and half are tenters.

Human and Natural History

On nearby Fort George Island is the restored Kingsley Plantation. This is an actual location where the famous Sea Island cotton was grown. The cotton was especially high in quality, and the flat seeds were easily separated from the fiber—important in pre-cotton-gin days. These two factors made Sea Island cotton the most profitable of all cottons to grow. But it took a lot of work, and this was why slave labor was so highly valued.

On the Kingsley Plantation are the remains of twenty-three of the original thirty-two slave cabins. In these cabins, slaves lived out their lives when they weren't working under the task system. Under the task system, slaves were given a specific amount of work to do every day, usually in the context of quarter-acre plots. When they completed their tasks they could pursue personal endeavors, such as tending their own gardens. The plantation owner would trade or sell these crops for the slaves.

Additional plantation jobs were divvied out under the task system. This system was unique to the rice-and cotton-growing Sea Islands. Other sections of the South used slave labor in "gangs," where a driver who was also a slave led the gang during the long day, with little personal time left over.

In the main house is a visitor center where artifacts found on the site are on display. You can also get a glimpse into the life of the plantation owner, Zephaniah Kingsley. He and his family operated the plantation from 1812 to 1854. The plantation was first established in 1791 by a man named McQueen.

In addition to the Kingsley home, there is also a restored barn on the site. As you drive away, imagine the sandy road as it was, with mature palm trees lining the road, which ran through cleared fields growing Sea Island cotton.

What To Do

Little Talbot and the surrounding islands are oriented toward nature lovers. The beach is foot-access only and makes for a fine place to relax or go beachcombing. The gradual depth changes along the oceanfront make for good swimming. The further north you head the more isolated the beach becomes. A good way to combine the beach with the woods is to take the Little Talbot Island Hiking Trail from near the ranger station two and a half miles through a lush maritime forest, passing some big dunes just before reaching the beach. From here you can head toward the north point or complete your loop by heading south on the beach to the first boardwalk. The Campground Nature Trail, which runs along an estuary of the Fort George River, makes for a good warm-up walk.

Canoeing is very popular on the back side of the island. Myrtle and Simpson creeks are paddling avenues of exploration for seeing wildlife in the grassy estuary. You can also bring your rod and fish for sea trout, redfish, and flounder. Surf fishermen will cast in the Atlantic for bigger species.

Ecotourists and birdwatchers will love Little Talbot. There are 194 species of birds known to inhabit the beaches, dunes, and estuaries of the park. Armadillo, raccoon, deer, rabbits, and bobcats are four-footed creatures that call this place home.

Another must-visit for nature lovers is the Black Rock Trail on Big Talbot Island. Walk through a level forest of live oak and then come to "The Bluffs." Descend onto the beach and explore the environs around Nassau Island. This is a great place to watch the sun rise and set. This new state acquisition is slated for more nature-friendly development sometime in the future. Long Island, which sits between Big and Little Talbot islands, is set to be made user-friendly as well.

What's Nearby

The best thing to do nearby is see Fort George Island. It is four miles south of Little Talbot on A1A. There you can walk, drive, or bike the 4.4-mile Saturiwa Trail. It is an old sandy road that makes a loop. This trail explores the human and natural history of the island. There are twenty-eight marked sites that explain the various periods of occupation from the time of the Saturiwa Indians to the plantation era to the modern era. The highlight of the loop is the Kingsley Plantation, which is maintained by the National Park Service. Make sure to get a handout at the Little Talbot ranger station before you attempt this trail.

There is a convenience store in the hamlet of Fort George four miles south of Little Talbot, but the only nearby full-service grocery and discount store is seventeen miles north in Fernandina Beach. If you want good seafood, head south to Fort George and cross the ferry to the fishing village of Mayport. There are restaurants there that serve seafood fresh off the boat. There are also some seafood restaurants on the Fort George side of the ferry.

Anastasia State Recreation Area

This state recreation area has three positive elements going for it: a very attractive campground set in a maritime hammock forest, miles of wide Atlantic Beach, and proximity to the historic heart of America's oldest city, St. Augustine.

Situated on Anastasia Island across the Bridge of Lions from downtown St. Augustine, this park lets you mix nature, a little watery recreation, and a trip through history without spending much time in your vehicle. And because Anastasia is on a spit of land branching off the main island, the beach and woodlands exude a natural feel that is surprising considering its proximity to downtown.

Sea, sand, and dunes on a foggy morn at Anastasia.

Key Information

Anastasia State Recreation Area
1340-A A1A South
St. Augustine, FL 32084
(904) 461-2033

Sites: 104 electric, 35 nonelectric

Amenities: Picnic table, fire ring, water spigot

Registration: By phone or at park entrance booth

Facilities: Hot showers, flush toilets, pay phone, laundry

Fees: $14 per night October–February, $16 per night March–
September, $2 electricity

Directions: From St. Augustine, drive south on A1A over the Bridge
of Lions for four miles. Anastasia State Recreation Area will be on
your left.

Set up camp beneath live oaks and magnolias in large campsites.
Then walk or drive your vehicle onto the beach, spread your stuff
out, and watch the waves roll in. After your day in the sun, head
into St. Augustine for an evening walking tour and a nice dinner.
Or just enjoy the evening at the campground and take a moonlit
stroll on the beach and see the historic sights of St. Augustine the
next day.

The Beach/Coast

Over four and a half miles of beach stretch along the northeastern
tip of Anastasia Island. The most northerly point of the island
overlooks the main entrance to St. Augustine Harbor. A jetty extends into the pass and is popular with fishermen. Beyond the

jetty is an inlet known as Salt Run, which has a small beach of its own. Salt Run nearly divides the spit from the rest of Anastasia Island.

Enter the shoreline from the beach parking area at the southern end of the recreation area. A sand road cuts through the dunes; this is how autos enter the beach. To your south is a beach area that is somewhat rocky and that goes a short distance to the park border. No cars are allowed here.

To your north begins the wide, gently sloping beach bordering the Atlantic Ocean, with the waves rolling in. Between the ocean and the dunes is the beach area where cars are allowed. Between this and the dunes is a roped-off area for people only. This way, sunbathers and families can relax without worrying about cars. Behind this are low dunes covered with sea oats.

The first mile of the beach is designated for swimmers only. This is the most popular area, since those who park off the beach walk to this location. The second mile of wide beach is the designated surfing area. The third and fourth miles of the beach, where the dunes flatten out, are designated for fishermen and personal watercraft. This setup allows like-minded beach enthusiasts to group together, minimizing conflicts.

In addition to this beach, there are a total of forty-two miles of beaches in St. Johns County. To the north is Vilano Beach, and to the south are St. Augustine Beach, Butler Beach, Crescent Beach, and Guana River State Park. Guana River has both beach and bayfront water access. A spectacular preserved beach is at Fort Matanzas, about ten miles south of Anastasia.

The Campground

This large campground is spread out in a beautiful maritime hammock forest. Thousands of years ago, when the ocean was higher than today, the site of the campground was covered in sand dunes and sea oats. But the ocean retreated and the rolling dunes became wooded. Now, the dominant tree, live oak, spreads its arms over southern magnolias, smaller oaks, cedar, palms, and a bushy, thick understory of yaupon, red bay, and young trees. Overhead, the tree canopy is sculpted by the constant action of wind coming off the Atlantic, which is a few hundred yards distant, divided from the campground by Salt Run. Old dunes give vertical variety to the campground.

Pass the small camp store on a sandy road and come to the first loop, Coquina. It is located away from the rest of the campground and has thirty-three campsites. A wide sandy road makes a lazy oval beneath a maritime hammock a little less thick than the rest of the campground. The campsites are very large and attract primarily RV campers.

The other six loops are on the main campground road. This road is sandy also, like all the campground roads. The first loop you pass is Sea Bean. This loop has water only, and lantern posts, which the electric sites do not have. It has fourteen smaller campsites in thick woods. Six of the sites are on a spur road of their own. Tenters prefer this loop as well as the next loop, Queen Conch. This loop also has water only, and the lantern posts. There are seventeen sites along this hilly loop, and a fully equipped bathhouse that is shared with the Sea Bean Loop.

Pass a small playground and come to Shark Eye Loop. The sites are bigger here and usually have a mix of all kinds of campers. The woods here are as attractive as the rest of the campground. Coupled with the Shark Eye Loop is the Sand Dollar Loop. It has fifteen campsites and a bathhouse shared with the Shark Eye Loop. The Sand Dollar campsites are spread even farther apart than the rest of the campground, which already has superior campsite privacy.

The last two loops are Sea Urchin and Angel Wing. These feature the same narrow oval design as the previous four loops. There are thirty-four campsites between them, and they share a common bathhouse.

These seven loops are spread widely over the campground. The thick woods overhead and the understory between the campsites make for a pleasant camping experience that is enhanced by the campground's cleanliness. All these factors make this an ever more popular place to park your rig or pitch your tent. The "off" season is from October through February, but even then weekend nights can fill. Spring and summer are very popular. Anastasia can be full every night during summer. Get reservations during this time.

Human and Natural History

In the mid-1500s, when Europeans were racing to gain control of the New World and its resources, France attempted to set up a colony a little north of Anastasia on the St. Johns River. One Don Pedro Menéndez de Avilés was sent from Spain to destroy the settlement and make his own colony. With the aid of a big storm the French settlement was abandoned. Menéndez then founded St. Augustine in the year 1565. Of course, the Timucuan Indians were already here.

Other European powers saw the value of Florida, which Juan Ponce de León had first sighted and named "Pascua Florida" in 1513. Later on, the English attacked St. Augustine no less than four times. These attacks prompted the construction of St. Augustine's famous Castillo de San Marcos. This fort, twenty-three years in the making, was built of a local sedimentary rock called coquina. During the 1702 attack, the fort was the only thing that didn't fall to the British, who burned the rest of the city. In 1763, British efforts finally paid off when they obtained Florida from the Spaniards in exchange for what is known today as Cuba.

The English ruled St. Augustine for only twenty years, but descendants of indentured servants brought here form a strong ethnic part of the town. St. Augustine was returned to the Spaniards but the Greek and Italian servants of the English stayed on. The United States obtained Florida from the Spanish in 1821. During the Civil War first Confederate, then Union forces occupied the fort and town.

After the war, oil man and Florida developer Henry Flagler came to town, building grand hotels and churches, visualizing St. Augustine as a major winter resort. His influence enhanced the old city. In 1924, Castillo de San Marcos was designated a national monument.

What To Do

The beach is the primary attraction at Anastasia. This is the only state park that permits beach driving. The sandy shoreline is wide and flat, with plenty of room for both man and machine. Most people park their cars and sunbathe and swim in the rolling Atlantic. During the warmer months a concessionaire rents all sorts of equipment, such as volleyballs, sailboards, and paddleboats.

The rolling waves of the Atlantic attract many surfers to the park. Personal watercraft are also permitted. Fishermen can surf cast on the beach for bluefish or pompano or fish the quieter waters of Salt Run for flounder or redfish. Salt Run is also where canoeists and sailboarders can be found. Both canoes and sailboards are for rent at Salt Run.

Before you walk around in St. Augustine, walk the Ancient Sand Dunes Nature Trail and see what this area was like before the Spaniards arrived. When you get to St. Augustine, park your vehicle near the visitor center and strike out from there. Cross the street and check out Castillo de San Marcos. Then take one of the sightseeing trains for an overview of the old town.

As you will see, the attractions are numerous. You can go the historic route and see the oldest wooden schoolhouse or get wacky and see the Ripley's Believe It or Not Museum. Or see the St. Augustine Alligator Farm, which has been around for more than a hundred years. That has to be a record for oldest tourist attraction. Climb the St. Augustine Lighthouse for a panoramic view of the surrounding environs.

Shoppers will need restraint in St. Augustine. There are rows of small galleries selling everything from crafts by skilled artisans to the cheapest plastic souvenirs.

What's Nearby

Beach lovers will want to explore the vast array of sandy shorelines extending both north and south. I highly recommend a trip south to Fort Matanzas National Monument. Not only does it have a dune and pristine sea oat beach, it has a Spanish fort from the 1740s located out in the entrance of the Matanzas River, which was the back way into St. Augustine. A free national park ferry boat takes you out to the fort itself. Just south of Fort Matanzas is the Washington Oaks State Gardens, where there are nearly four hundred acres of scenic, rock-strewn beach and ornamental gardens to see.

Since Anastasia is so close to St. Augustine, food and supplies are readily available no matter which way you turn. However, the Salt Run camp store is onsite at the campground.

There are many places to dine in town. One place to consider is Churchill's Attic, near the old fort. You can enjoy the atmosphere inside or out on the patio, which overlooks the water, while eating fare ranging from burgers to seafood. You'll probably end up accomplishing a combination of sightseeing, shopping, and eating in the true tourist style.

Gamble Rogers Memorial State Recreation Area

Beachfront camping is the major attraction here—and this is the last beachfront camping to be had between Flagler Beach and the Keys to the south. Located just south of the town of Flagler Beach, this small recreation area of only 144 acres packs a powerful punch. The Atlantic rises right up to the reddish-tan sands, which rise to a wind-sculpted grassy dune that is more like a bluff. Atop this bluff sits the campground. Across A1A is the rest of the park.

Use Gamble Rogers as a base camp to explore the other beaches of the area as well as the cultural and historic sights of this quiet Atlantic coastline. Nearby are county and state beaches, including one of the state's newest acquisitions, North Peninsula State Rec-

Boardwalk leading to orange sands by the Atlantic.

Key Information

Gamble Rogers Memorial Recreation Area at Flagler Beach
3100 South A1A
Flagler Beach, FL 32136
(904) 517-2086

Sites: 34

Amenities: Picnic table, fire ring, water spigot, electricity

Registration: By phone or at park entrance booth

Facilities: Hot showers, flush toilets, pay phone

Fees: $18 per night, $2 electricity

Directions: Gamble Rogers is just south of the pier in the town of Flagler Beach on Highway A1A.

reation Area. Farther inland are Bulow Creek State Park, home of the renowned Fairchild Oak, and the Bulow Plantation Ruins State Historic Site, where you can see relics of an old sugar mill and gain insight into life on a sugar plantation of the early 1800s.

The Beach/Coast

Since Gamble Rogers is limited in size, there is only about a quarter-mile of direct Atlantic coastline. The colorful sands are made of crushed shells pounded from the waves. These shells, when compacted, form a rock known as coquina, which means "little shell" in Spanish. The high bluff along this coast lies atop the coquina.

There is only about a hundred feet of beach between the Atlantic and where the salt spray–pruned grass and palmetto-covered dunes rise almost vertically, then level off on top of the coquina, which is also covered in low-lying dune vegetation. When you are below this bluff you feel almost closed in next to the Atlantic.

Two boardwalks lead down from the day-use parking area to the beach. There is an outdoor shower and an indoor bathhouse for day users. Moving southward along the beach, you will come to five other boardwalks that connect the beach to the campground. Such direct beach access from the campground is the big drawing card for Gamble Rogers.

The Intracoastal Waterway flows along the rear of the park on Smith Creek. There is a constructed aquatic entrance to the park from the waterway called Boat Basin. A picnic area with covered pavilions lies along Boat Basin.

Just a few miles south is the North Peninsula State Recreation Area. Here you have an uninterrupted two-and-a-half-mile stretch of beach to enjoy. Beachcombers can stretch their legs and watch the coast melt away in the distance. North of Gamble Rogers is Flagler Beach and the city pier, where many people fish. Farther north is Beverly Beach and the rocky coastline at Washington Oaks State Gardens.

The Campground

You are one with the ocean at this campground. On a windy or stormy day the waves sound like they are going to come over the bluff and wash out the campground. But the fact that it is a good thirty or forty feet from the campground down to the water should alleviate that concern.

This is an intimate campground, with only thirty-four camp-sites sandwiched between the Atlantic and Highway A1A. Overhead, there is little vegetation, save for a few palm trees on the inland side of the campground. The rest of the vegetation is salt-pruned grasses and palmetto. Ocean breezes come easy, which keeps the insects down in the warmer months, but also keeps a chill on when the weather is cool.

The campsites themselves are sand bordered with grass and co-quina rocks. The campsites are numbered with big coquina rocks planted in the sand. Between the campsites are thickets of dense palmetto standing about four to six feet high, creating decent campsite barriers, but no shade.

As you pass the locked campground gate, you pass campsites on either side of the sandy road. Campsite barriers are very thick here. Pass a boardwalk leading to the ocean after Campsite 5. There is another boardwalk after Campsite 11. The vegetation falls away on the sea side, revealing a nice ocean view. Come to the bathhouse with indoor and outdoor showers. The bathhouse also has a beach boardwalk.

Past the bathhouse and dump station are ten more campsites. The palmetto is thick here, then tapers off dramatically, becoming scant thereafter. You get glimpses of A1A, complete views of your neighbors, and wide-open ocean vistas. Then the campground ends in a vehicle turnaround.

The openness of the campground discourages many tent camp-ers. However, if you find the right site, you could hunker down behind a palmetto thicket and be just fine. It is generally windier here in the winter, so tent campers may be better off at Gamble Rogers in the summer. RV campers will find the large sites much to their liking. They can park their rigs and have plenty of room to set out the lawn chairs. And when the wind blows they can simply escape inside.

Gamble Rogers has become more popular over the years. It is a year-round recreation location. Once March rolls around you can expect a full house every night until September. Make reservations this time of year. Things calm down in early fall, then from De-cember on the cold weather sends the snowbirds south, though weeknights offer a few open campsites.

Human and Natural History

The Bulow Plantation Historic Site contains the remnants of an old sugar mill that is very worth your time to tour. In the 1820s Charles Bulow cleared 2,200 acres of land along the creek that now bears his name, planting sugarcane among other crops. His son John took over the plantation after the elder Bulow's death, and it took off.

Sugarcane was processed into sugar. You can walk the remains of the sugar mill today and understand the process. Cane was planted in January and was ready for harvest by mid-October. The woods you see all around you were once fields. First the cane was cut in those fields, and then it was brought to the mill and placed on a conveyor. A boiler-powered engine operated rollers that crushed the cane. The cane juice then fell into settling vats, while the leftover cane, called "bagasse," was hauled away. The cane juice flowed from vats on the top floor into a series of five kettles. Then the juice was hand-dipped from larger to smaller kettles and ended up as a syrup.

When the syrup reached "strike" stage it was put in large wooden cooling vats to harden. Then the solid product was cut up and placed into wooden barrels. The barrels were then loaded onto wagons and taken to a boat landing where the sugar was shipped off to St. Augustine or Jacksonville.

The Second Seminole War ended the plantation's heyday in 1836, as it was burned by the Indians after John Bulow fled the area. This is ironic because Bulow was against the policy of removing the Seminoles from Florida to the West. There are also remains of the plantation house, a spring house, wells, and a small museum that displays artifacts found at the site.

What To Do

Walking directly from your campsite to the ocean is one of the best things to do at Gamble Rogers. So is watching an Atlantic sunrise. Many people will just plop right down on a beach chair, watch the sun make its way across the sky, and maybe get in the water a time or two to cool off. It's all about relaxation. If you want to beachcomb, go down to the North Peninsula Recreation Area. Beverly Beach is less busy than the beach around the Flagler Beach pier. Beachcombers may also want to head north to see the gardens and rocky shoreline of Washington Oaks.

Surf fishermen can set up their rods on the beach for whiting, pompano, or bluefish, or cast in the Intracoastal Waterway for flounder and redfish. Or they can go up to the Flagler Beach pier. There is a boat launch on the Intracoastal Waterway. If you don't have a boat, walk the nature trail that meanders through a coastal scrub community in the narrow park.

It is just a short drive to the Bulow Plantation Ruins State Historic Site. Get directions at Gamble Rogers park office. Not only can you tour the ruins, you can take the four-mile Bulow Woods Hiking Trail, which leads into a shady oak hammock among live oak trees and along Bulow Creek and near a marsh before looping back to the parking area.

Bulow Creek is a state-designated canoe trail. There is a landing at the state historic site and canoes available for rent. You can paddle upstream for three miles or head down six miles to the Intracoastal Waterway. The tidal marsh and surrounding lush woods make for a memorable paddle. Anglers can vie for both freshwater and saltwater species.

What's Nearby

Another recent state acquisition is Bulow Creek State Park. It is a forest enclave along the west shore of Bulow Creek. Here grows the Fairchild Oak, a rare example of an ideally shaped old-growth live oak that has not fallen prey to development or fire. There is a three-mile hiking trail that connects the Fairchild Oak to the Bulow Woods Trail, creating a six-mile, one-way hike between the Fairchild Oak and the Bulow Plantation Ruins State Historic Site. I recommend that you make this hike during the cooler and drier winter months.

A full-service grocery store is located in Flagler Beach near I-95. There are two excellent seafood restaurants in Flagler Beach. The first is High Tides Snack Jack. Bring cash because they don't take credit cards. The other is the Fisherman's Net—a restaurant and seafood market where you can get lunch or dinner.

Tomoka State Park

Tomoka has the good fortune of having one of the state's most attractive campgrounds and the good fortune of being located minutes away from the world's most famous beach, Daytona. Tucked away on the north tip of the peninsula between the Halifax and Tomoka Rivers, Tomoka reeks of remoteness yet is within the boundaries of the city of Ormond Beach. Ormond Beach and Daytona Beach are a ten-minute drive from your favorite campsite at Tomoka.

But you'll have a difficult time picking out your favorite campsite. Mother Nature mixed in a little north and a little south Florida then placed it near the ocean, resulting in a junglelike forest that belies the actual location of this suburban getaway. The

Ormond Beach, near Tomoka.

Timucuan Indians thought highly of Tomoka Point as well. In pre-Columbian days, the village of Nocoroco stood here. The natives lived off the rich estuarine waters of the surrounding lagoon. An onsite museum tells all about the history of the Timucuans. So you can enjoy a day at the beach and maybe learn a little history too.

The Beach/Coast

Tomoka is surrounded on three sides by water. The Tomoka River flows from the west into Tomoka Basin, where it meets the Halifax River, which is the body of water between the mainland and the barrier island occupying Ormond Beach. The peninsula housing the state park has small barrier islands and inlets surrounding it, so most of your views are of nature, not condos. Off in the distance are grassy salt marshes and cedar- and palm-lined coast leading right up to the estuary, though there is a short stretch of beach on the northwest end of the peninsula.

But just a short drive away at the end of Granada Street is the real beach and the Atlantic Ocean. Here you pass an access booth then turn right onto the beach. The light-tan sands rise moderately from the ocean and then into a steep bluff. On top of the bluff are numerous houses, condos, and hotels.

Down on the beach is a long line of poles between the ocean and the developments. These poles restrict automotive access. If you are behind the poles you need not worry about autos. North of Granada Street the beach is blocked off from auto traffic. This is a conservation area where you are free to fly your kite or walk around without worrying about traffic.

This Ormond Beach access is the first of several beach-access points maintained by Volusia County. Farther south lies Daytona, the world's most famous beach. This notoriety attracts beach lovers of all types. Teenagers come here as a rite of passage. Other folks come to relax or indulge in watery pursuits. Others come to watch the other people. Daytona is a great beach to see humanity at play.

The Campground

I can confidently say that Tomoka has one of the five most attractive campgrounds in the state. Of course this is a matter of opinion, but if you like to camp amidst the natural world, where campground amenities are integrated into a wooded setting rather than vice versa, then you will agree with me.

The backbone of the forest here is live oak. Resurrection ferns and Spanish moss thrive on this host tree. Oak limbs stretch over the balance of the forest, which is also heavy with palm trees.

These palms add to the tropical feel of Tomoka. Smaller scrub oaks fill the woods, along with pine trees. The heavy understory allows campers ample privacy.

Enter the sandy one-way campground loop road and pass the first eleven campsites, all on the outside of the loop. The waters of a small inlet are faintly visible in the background. Pass the Visitors Program Building, a good rainy-day refuge, on your left, then come to a group of campsites laid out along both sides of the road. Heavy vegetation takes care of any privacy issues at these campsites, which all have water and electricity. There is ample room at all the campsites.

Past Campsite 34 are water-only campsites. This is the de facto tent campground. All the sites are on the outside of the loop, with the exception of a few sites along a road bisecting the main campground loop. Some campsites here are very close to the inlet waters. By now, you will be noticing how clean this place is. The park staffers take pride in keeping this campground tidy.

Curve around the loop and pass more water-only sites until you reach Campsite 70. Then the water and electricity sites begin again. RV campers will be comfortable parking their rigs among the magnolias here. Some of the sites have a little less vegetation by Tomoka standards and are delineated with wooden barriers.

Due to the thickness of the vegetation, you will see only a few of your fellow campers if any, making the campground seem small. And after a sun-splashed day at the beach, I appreciate a shady campsite. Three bathhouses keep the walk from your tent or RV to the shower minimal.

Tomoka is fairly quiet during January, with some snowbirds setting up camp. But in February watch out. During "Speed Week" at the Daytona Speedway, campers fill up the place to the gills. So it goes during "Bike Week," when motorcycle enthusiasts fill the streets of nearby Daytona. Then the spring breakers come, but they usually don't fill the campground completely. Campsites are generally available during summer, except for major holidays. After September, business slows again until cold weather infiltrates the northland. Any time of year is a good time to visit Tomoka.

Human and Natural History

The Timucuan Indians were part of the first group of Indians to enter Florida over fourteen thousand years ago. A band of Timucuans settled in a village known as Nocoroco on the western end of the peninsula that today is Tomoka State Park. There the Timucuans could harvest the rich waters of Tomoka Basin and be protected from hurricanes by the barrier island where Ormond Beach is today.

Oyster mounds and burial mounds at the park are important archaeological sites, with some archaeological evidence dating back seven thousand years. Timucuan communities were often located within wooden walls not unlike a fort. Within the refuge was a central community house where the chief lived, with smaller huts for individual citizens nearby.

The sea was not their only food source. The Timucuans were also skilled hunters, using the bow and arrow as well as traps. Deer and small game complemented their seafood diet. By the mid-1700s the Timucuans were all but wiped out by European colonization.

One colonizer was a Scot by the name of Richard Oswald. Oswald received a grant from the British government that included the lands where the village of Nocoroco once stood. Oswald arranged for people and provisions and began to turn Tomoka Point into Mount Oswald, a growing plantation with a modest main house, slave quarters, and outbuildings. Oswald himself mainly stayed across the ocean, leaving the operation to hired hands. Indigo, used to make a deep blue dye, was the primary crop.

As the plantation grew, oranges, timber, and rice were exported to England from Mount Oswald. Oswald later played an important part in the peace negotiations between the British and Americans at the close of the Revolutionary War. Mount Oswald later fell into decline. The only signs of Oswald's operation that remain are drainage canals in the tidal marshes.

What To Do

Tomoka is only a short drive to either Ormond or Daytona Beach. At Ormond Beach you have the option of going to an auto-accessible beach or a foot-only beach. Either way, the Atlantic Ocean is its same beautiful self, ebbing and flowing day and night, waiting patiently for your arrival. As you head toward Daytona Beach a wider variety of concessionaires will rent you the equipment to jet ski, sail, surf, or whatever floats your body. The city of Daytona Beach also has all manner of tourist fun, such as miniature golf and so forth.

After a day at the beach, you will appreciate the wooded environment of Tomoka. Park rangers tell me that relaxing at the campground is a time-honored pastime here. But if you want to keep on the move, bear in mind that Tomoka has a little waterfront of its own. But do your swimming at the beach, as it is not allowed at the park. What you can do is take a walk on the nature trail. It starts near the park museum. The park museum interprets the rich human history that has been played out on Tomoka Point. It also houses artworks of Fred Dana Marsh, including the sculpture "Legend of Tomokie." Marsh was a multitalented artist who settled in Ormond Beach in the 1920s. The sculpture was his last project.

Boating and canoeing are popular in the Tomoka and Halifax Rivers. There is a boat launch at the park. Since the park is surrounded on three sides by water, angling for the sea trout, flounder, and snook that inhabit the brackish depths is popular.

What's Nearby

Since Tomoka is a suburban park, civilization is only a short drive away. Any type of store or restaurant is handy. In the search for seafood follow this general rule: get as close to fishing villages or fishing boats as possible; if there are no fishing boats or villages nearby, then get as close to the ocean as possible. This axiom is not infallible, but it will help more than it hurts.

State holdings nearby include the Fairchild Oak and Bulow Plantation Ruins. The former is an ancient, near-perfect live oak specimen, and the latter is the site of a plantation and old sugar mill that is very worth the drive. Canoers can paddle three canoe trails, at Bulow Creek, Spruce Creek, and the upper reaches of the Tomoka River. The sights of Cape Canaveral Space Center and Cape Canaveral National Seashore are a reasonable drive to the south.

☼ Central Florida

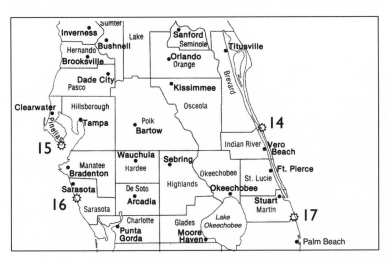

Detail area

14   Sebastian Inlet State Recreation Area

15   Fort De Soto County Park

16   Oscar Scherer State Park

17   Jonathan Dickinson State Park

Surfers at Sebastian Inlet.

Sebastian Inlet State Recreation Area

This region of Florida is known as the Treasure Coast. It was named after the offshore sinking of a Spanish fleet laden with gold and gems from Mexico, South America, and the Orient. To-day, Sebastian Inlet is a natural gem among the gold and jewels that lie hidden beneath the Atlantic waves. The south end of the park harbors the McLarty Treasure Museum, which contains artifacts from the infamous decimated Spanish fleet that sank.

A Mecca for water sports, specifically fishing and surfing, Sebastian Inlet was developed with ocean lovers in mind. More

---

☼

Key Information

Sebastian Inlet State Recreation Area
9700 South A I A
Melbourne Beach, FL 32951
(407) 984-4852

Sites: 51 water and electric, 3 other

Amenities: Picnic table, fire ring

Registration: By phone or at park entrance booth

Facilities: Hot showers, flush toilets, pay phone, laundry

Fees: $13 per night May–November, $17 per night December–April, $2 electricity

Directions: From Vero Beach head east on State Road 60 to US A I A. Turn left on A I A and head north for about ten miles to Sebastian Inlet State Recreation Area.

---

than four miles of unspoiled beach face the strong Atlantic waves, where surfers try to "hang ten." The waves here are among the best on the entire east coast. Other park visitors indulge in less strenuous pursuits, like watching the surfers. Jetties, piers, a bait store, and a marina make fishing here very user-friendly.

Ecotourism is on the rise here also, with the proximity of Pelican Island, America's oldest wildlife refuge, and the Archie Carr National Wildlife Refuge, America's newest wildlife refuge. Much of the park also abuts the Indian River Lagoon, North America's most diverse estuary. Ranger-led tours leave the park marina daily in search of the birds and mammals of this natural treasure.

The Beach/Coast

Because Sebastian Inlet is located on Orchid Island, a barrier island, nearly the entire park is surrounded by coastline. The actual Sebastian Inlet was redredged in 1947. The original cut connecting the Indian River with the Atlantic was made in 1918. So the park is divided into two sections. Starting in the north, two miles from the inlet, Atlantic beach rises fairly sharply from the blue waters. Usually a level bench of sand marks the high-tide line. Behind the tan sand is a low-slung maritime forest. This lovely stretch of beach continues to the inlet, where two jetties banked with rocks protect the inlet from filling in. This "real Florida" beach continues south of the inlet, offering ample space for everyone.

The west side of the barrier island is primarily mangrove bordering the rich Indian River Lagoon, which has an average depth of three feet. The mangrove shoreline twists and turns, overlooking smaller mangrove islands, then returns north to the inlet again. In times of strong tide, water positively rushes through the pass with incredible force. But the sea wall is down in one area of the inlet, and a small pool rises and lowers with the tide. Here park visitors bring their children to swim in safety. North of the inlet, the mangrove resumes its winding form and eventually comes to Inlet Marina, run by a state park concessionaire.

The Campground

The campground is located on a small peninsula between Sebastian Inlet and a small tidal lagoon of Indian River. This setup makes for some decent bug-ridding ocean breezes. Since part of the dredge spoils from the inlet were dumped here, the campground, built on part of the dredge mound, is hilly by Florida standards. Campground vegetation is somewhat sparse, but restorative planting by park personnel after removing exotic vegetation is taking hold. Sea grape, gumbo limbo, cabbage palm, and cedar will eventually provide better cover than exists today.

Three rows of campsites are situated along two loops. As you enter the campground, the first loop has twenty sites on a small elongated knoll overlooking the Indian River. These campsites are the least vegetated and are the smallest, yet RVers manage to park their rigs and still have room for folding chairs and the like. If you favor a good view, stay in this row.

The second row of campsites is in the middle of the campground. It lies in a somewhat more vegetated area. In addition to planted trees, brush such as privet and salt myrtle break up the campsites, which are medium to small in size. Low-lying board barriers have been erected to delineate some of the more open sites. Of special note are three tent-only campsites on the west end of this row; these sites do not have electricity or water. Water is available from the nearby bathhouses.

Moving southward, a large area planted in native vegetation is growing up around two bathhouses, each with hot showers, flush toilets, a laundry, and a phone. Behind this, a third row of campsites lies next to a thick growth of mangrove bordering a tidal lagoon. These fifteen campsites are on natural ground and are low lying compared to the rest of the campground. Divided by planted natural vegetation, these sites are by far the largest, with adequate room for any RV or the largest tent-camping family or group. The price of having no view is what you pay to stay in one of these sites.

Sebastian Inlet is enjoying increasing popularity and is busier than ever. Generally, campsite composition is three to one in favor of RVs during winter. Reverse that during the summer. The campground will be full of snowbirds between December and mid-April. Summer weekends and holidays can fill too. Get reservations during this time. I didn't have reservations in January and had to put my name on a waiting list, but I was lucky enough to get the last campsite available.

Human and Natural History

When Spain was a world power its sailors scoured the world, plundering it for riches. After gathering treasures from what is now Mexico and Peru, Spanish ships would meet in Cuba to sail en masse back to Spain. The long journey northward along the Florida coast was always dangerous, but on one fateful day in August 1715, no amount of armament would have helped. A hurricane sank an entire fleet of ships on that August day. More than a thousand men washed up on shore, only to face the glaring sun and relentless insects. They feared the Indians, too. But the Ais Indians actually gave them food. The natives saw that the land was rich with fish, turtles, and manatees from the sea and deer, bear, and wild plants from the land. Yet many sailors died waiting for salvagers from Havana. The salvagers recovered only half of the loot. The rest lay at the bottom of the sea, buried by shifting sands beneath the waves.

Then, in the 1950s another hurricane struck the area, altering the coastline and exposing the salvagers' camp, located where the McLarty Museum is today. Next, a fellow named Kip Wagner found one of the ships, and treasure hunters donned scuba gear and hit the mother lode—gold bars, doubloons, and jewelry as well as more archaeologically significant artifacts that provided a window into the everyday world of the Spanish sailor. These artifacts are on display at the McLarty Museum.

What To Do

Surfers take on the waves year-round. In the winter, when the waves are bigger, they can be seen in wetsuits paddling out on their boards just north of the inlet. Now, for most of us surfing is not on the menu, but even if you don't surf, walk out on the north jetty and watch them try to ride the waves, sometimes going a long way, sometimes crashing in an eruption of white foam.

But just about everyone can fish, and there are so many places to fish here! With an onsite tackle and bait shop, it's even easier. And the fishing is so good. The primary place to angle is from one of the two jetties along the inlet. Bait buckets beside them, anglers toss lines off the jetty railing or take seats on the huge rocks against the jetty.

Below the bridge spanning the inlet are two catwalks that extend into the inlet. Other fishermen will be surf fishing there. Others will be trying their luck in the Indian River Lagoon. And for those with boats, the options range out to the sea, farther out in the lagoon and beyond. The park marina here makes having a boat a piece of cake.

It's at the park marina where you can rent canoes, kayaks, and motorboats to tool around Indian River Lagoon and explore the wildlife refuge. This is also where you can take the ranger-led cruise aboard the Inlet Explorer and see what birds and sea creatures turn up in the Indian River Lagoon. Depending upon the time of year you may spot dolphins, manatees, sea turtles, and any manner of birds.

With more than four miles of beach right on the Atlantic, you can walk the tan sand until your feet shrivel. But if you lie still, don't be surprised to find yourself lulled into a nap by the crashing waves. If you get tired of walking the sand, take the park nature trail and learn about the maritime forest of this protected barrier island.

What's Nearby

North of the Treasure Coast is what's known as the Space Coast. About an hour north of Sebastian Inlet is the Cape Canaveral area. Here you can go to the astronaut hall of fame and enjoy other celestial diversions. Nature lovers have the Cape Canaveral National Seashore to enjoy.

Some minor supplies can be purchased at the park bait shop, but you must travel ten miles north of Sebastian Inlet to find a full-service grocery store. Near the north jetty is a snack bar serving burgers and hot dogs. Two restaurants of note are located south toward Vero Beach. The Ocean Grill has reliably good seafood. The Pearl Bistro offers a varied menu with a Caribbean touch.

Fort De Soto County Park

Located just south of the Tampa Bay urban complex, Fort De Soto County Park is a beach camper's getaway located on a chain of small islands dominated by Mullet Key. I found out about this well-manicured and well-run preserve through word of mouth and visualized an overrun, beaten down, has-been island ruined by its proximity to St. Petersburg. Was I ever wrong. Pinellas County has done a fantastic job making this short-lived military base into a getaway for beach lovers.

Fort De Soto features a well-groomed campground that is divided into three sections, with separate areas for tent and RV campers. Nearly three out of every four campsites offers an ocean

The author at his beachfront campsite.

Key Information

Fort De Soto County Park
631 Chestnut Street
Clearwater, FL 34616-5336
(813) 866-2662

Sites: 233

Amenities: Picnic table, standup grill, water spigot, electricity, lantern post

Registration: At park office

Facilities: Hot showers, flush toilets, pay phone, laundry

Fees: $18.75 per night

Directions: From St. Petersburg head south on I-275 to State Road 682. Head east on 682 to Pinellas Bayway, 679. Turn left on Pinellas Bayway and dead-end into Fort De Soto County Park.

view. A large staff keeps the campground as well as the entire park very tidy.

The beaches of Mullet Key offer fantastic views of the Tampa Bay and Gulf area. The beachside accommodations match those views. Recreation opportunities are numerous and include beachcombing, canoeing, hiking, biking, and fishing. The park makes recreation very user-friendly. Beach campers will not be disappointed if they come to Fort De Soto County Park. It offers the best beach camping anyone could ask for near an urban setting.

The Beach/Coast

Cross the bridge over Bunces Pass and you are on the chain of islands comprising De Soto, located at the entrance of Tampa Bay. Madeline Key leads onto St. Jean Key. A short bridge crosses over to the main campground on St. Christopher Key. The main road comes to Mullet Key, a V-shaped island that encompasses most of the park and that has all of that fantastic beach. Off Mullet Key is Boone Fortune Key. Some of the smaller islands have been connected to one another with fill.

Madeline Key has the park boat ramp and looks northward toward the mainland. It and St. Christopher and St. Jean Key are inside the "V" of Mullet Key in Mullet Key Bayou. Some of your views from these keys are of Mullet Key or other small islands, not of the park. You'll find beach areas, but their shorelines are primarily mangrove.

The inner areas of Mullet Key are also made up of mangrove, forming a harbor of greenery. But the outside of Mullet Key is all beach. The eastern edge of the key looks into Tampa Bay and the Sunshine Skyway, the road that crosses southward from St. Petersburg into Manatee County. The mainland is in the distance.

More than seven miles of beach line the southern edge of the island. The East Beach Swim Area is a designated swimming location. Pass more beach. Then come to the Bay Pier, which extends five hundred feet into Tampa Bay. Beyond the pier is Fort De Soto, located at the southern point of Mullet Key, which then turns north. You will immediately come to the thousand-foot Gulf Pier.

Beyond the pier, the north-running beach, good for shelling, looks over the Gulf of Mexico. The shoreline splits, and a sandy peninsula is divided by the North Beach Swim Area, which is a small inlet surrounded by sand and perfect for windy days and children. The island ends at the western edge of Bunces Pass.

The Campground

Park designers did a great job with this campground. It is divided into three well-landscaped camping areas. One camping area is on St. Jean Key, and the other two areas are on St. Christopher Key.

Pass the camp office and store, then turn left into Area I. This is the exclusive domain of tent, van, and pop-up campers. A gravel road cuts through a thick forest of live oak and palm growing out of a tangle of palmetto and other brush.

Fifty-six of the eighty-five campsites on this loop have an ocean view. Most have a view into Mullet Key Bayou. Others look over St. Jean Key. In most cases the woods have been cleared to make the most of the view. A larger grassy area parallels a small beach between the campsites and the water. In some cases a small sea wall has been constructed to prevent erosion. The other campsites face the center of the loop.

There are two modern bathhouses in the center of the loop. One feature of special interest to tent campers is the day room, which has tables, couches, and a large fireplace. This is a potential refuge on rainy, buggy, or very hot days.

Camp Area II is on St. Jean Key. It is for RV campers. Again, the most is made of the interface between land and sea, resulting in forty-two ocean-view sites. All of the campsites are in a thick wood of live oak and palm that is trimmed high, allowing tall motor homes to get in and out of the campsites without damaging their rigs. One row of campsites abuts the main park road, but thick vegetation provides adequate screening. Another row of campsites juts out into Mullet Key Bayou.

Camp Area III is back out on St. Christopher Key. It is also RV only and is the better of the two good RV camping areas. More than fifty of the seventy campsites have an ocean view. The ones that don't have a view are pull-through sites in the loop center that can accommodate extra-big rigs. Here, too, the attractive forest of live oak and palm has been trimmed to accommodate RVs. Two bathhouses serve this loop.

De Soto has some distinctive rules. The only valid forms of payment, for example, are cash and travelers' checks. You can make reservations only in person. The goal here is to keep campsites open for natives of Pinellas County. Plan your trip accordingly. If you have any questions at all, call ahead. The busy time at Fort De Soto is February through April. Campsites are generally available during the summer, except during major holidays, though summer weekends have been known to fill.

Human and Natural History

In Tampa Bay, like all of Florida, the Indians had a pretty good thing going until the Europeans arrived. Here the primary European explorer was none other than Mr. Hernando De Soto himself. In 1542 De Soto came to the southern shores of Tampa Bay, right near Mullet Key, and began his celebrated excursion over the southeast, searching for gold and the fountain of youth among other things.

Fast forward to the 1840s, when a group of U.S. Army engineers envisioned Mullet Key as the ideal location from which to defend Tampa Bay. They procured the key in the name of the U.S. government, preventing development until a fort named De Soto was constructed in 1900.

Guns and men were placed in this desolate location. Outbuildings were constructed. Then boredom and misery set in. Biting pests tormented the soldiers. There was simply nothing to do. Lives languished on this lonely key for nine years. Gradually, fewer and fewer soldiers were left to man the fort. During World War I, twenty-six men defended Tampa Bay from Fort De Soto. By 1923 there was only one soul occupying the whole fort.

The United States tried to sell the fort but couldn't get a decent bid. Then for a while the state of Florida had a quarantine station there. Are you getting the idea that this place was thought of as forsaken? To top it all, during World War II Mullet Key was turned into a bombing range!

Finally, Pinellas County obtained possession of the island chain and developed it as a park. The design was laid out—very well in my opinion—and the park was opened in 1963. In this age of slap-a-condo-everywhere-south-of-Orlando, Mullet Key and the surrounding islands surely would be built up but for the army engineers of 1849, who decided that it looked like a good place for a fort. And now we have the beach camper's nirvana of Fort De Soto. We must give some credit also to Pinellas County.

What To Do

Fun at Fort De Soto starts with the beach. More than seven miles of sandy shoreline, half facing Tampa Bay, half facing the Gulf of Mexico, await adventurers. This should help you find just the right combination of view, sun, and wind to suit your fancy. If you want to swim, enjoy the two developed beach areas, East Beach and North Beach. They both have picnic areas, bathroom facilities, and lifeguards in the summer. Some beach areas are posted no swimming. Heed the warnings, for there are some wicked currents flowing in and out of Tampa Bay.

Fishermen have all sorts of opportunities. You can surf fish or use one of the two piers. Each of these piers has a bait and snack shop. Or you can fish Mullet Key Bayou. You'll have to do so from a self-propelled craft, however, since most of the bayou is off limits to motorized travel. Canoers and kayakers can enjoy Mullet Key Bayou and a designated canoe trail winding through the mangrove. A concessionaire rents canoes. Motorboaters can use a large boat ramp near Bunces Pass on Madeline Key.

Near the Arrowhead Picnic Area is a nature trail that winds amid the habitats of the key. Once they arrive on the island, bicyclists, roller bladers, and hikers need not use their cars. A four-mile paved recreation trail connects all of the major features of the island, including Fort De Soto itself. At the stronghold you can take a self-guided tour. Make sure to climb to the upper portion of the fort. It offers a panoramic view of the entire Tampa Bay area. Of course, simple relaxation can take place anywhere, from your ocean-view campsite to a wide stretch of beach.

What's Nearby

Most beach campers will find this park fulfilling, but you may get the urge to explore the bay area. Two popular attractions are the Florida Aquarium and Busch Gardens. Busch Gardens is a combination theme park, zoo, museum, and entertainment complex just north of the city of Tampa Bay. The Florida Aquarium replicates the state's many aquatic environments, from freshwater springs to coral reefs. Shoreline habitats such as beaches and mangrove forests complete the picture at the aquarium.

Other nearby beaches located along a string of barrier islands extending north from Mullet Key are St. Pete Beach, Treasure Island Beach, and Madeira Beach. All of these beaches are run by Pinellas County.

Supplies can be obtained at the camp store near the campground entrance. All of the stores and restaurants an urban area could provide are just north of De Soto in the city of St. Petersburg.

Oscar Scherer State Park

Sarasota County is blessed with a lot of water. From the east flows the Myakka River and other freshwater streams that course toward the ocean. Sarasota's western border is the clear blue sea of the Gulf of Mexico. Oscar Scherer State Park lies just east of the Gulf on the brackish waters of South Creek. Here you can camp in the rich woods along South Creek and enjoy the nearby Gulf waters that abut the many beaches of Sarasota County. Oscar Scherer has many attractions centering around South Creek and Lake Osprey, a freshwater impoundment. A trip to Myakka River State Park, with

Shady campsite at Oscar Scherer.

✿

Key Information

Oscar Scherer State Park
1843 South Tamiami Trail
Osprey, FL 34229
(941) 483-5956

Sites: 104

Amenities: Picnic table, fire ring, water spigot, electricity

Registration: By phone or at park entrance booth

Facilities: Hot showers, flush toilets, pay phone

Fees: $11 per night May–November, $15 per night December–April, $2 electricity

Directions: Oscar Scherer State Park is just south of Osprey on US 41.

two lakes and the Myakka River within its twenty-eight thousand acres, completes your watery grand slam of Sarasota County.

It all starts at Oscar Scherer. Conveniently located on US 41, the Tamiami Trail, this state park acts as a bridge between fresh and salt water, and as a wildlife refuge in the fast-developing southwest Florida coast. And this high and dry pine flatwoods community is normally just the kind of terrain sought by developers.

Oscar Scherer was an inventor who developed a process for dyeing leather shoes. His daughter, Elsa Scherer Burrows, donated the 462 acres of the park to the state in 1955. The park opened in 1956. Another nine hundred acres was added in 1991. Because of Elsa's generosity, park visitors now enjoy this preserved piece of Sarasota County.

The Beach/Coast

South Creek flows through the center of the piney woods of the park. The forest is more lush and dense along the dark and silent stream. Palms and oaks draped with Spanish moss rise above the thickets of palmetto alongside the waterway, where the tide raises and lowers the water level. Just a few yards away from South Creek is Lake Osprey. This dammed freshwater lake with a small beach provides safe swimming opportunities for park visitors.

Beach lovers will be happy to know that no less than seven beaches lie within a short driving distance of Oscar Scherer. Most of these beaches are on narrow barrier islands that run north and south along the Gulf. The two primary barrier islands are Casey Key and Siesta Key. Swimming, fishing, beachcombing, and picnicking await you there. Most of these beaches are maintained by Sarasota County.

The closest beach to Oscar Scherer is Nokomis Beach on Casey Key. Weekends are busy, with people of all ages enjoying all manner of beach activities. Just south of Nokomis Beach is North Jetty Park. Here picnickers dine in the shade of Australian pines. Others are out on the crushed-shell seaside, and others are fishing from the jetty that protects Venice Inlet. Across Venice Inlet is Venice Municipal Beach and a fishing pier to enjoy. Farther south are Brohard Park Beach and Caspersen Park Beach on Manasota Key.

North of Oscar Scherer, on Siesta Key, are Siesta Key Beach Park and Turtle Beach. You could spend a day at each and decide for yourself which one is best.

The Campground

Oscar Scherer has a well-designed campground that utilizes the best of its setting. The result is an alluringly shady camping area stretched out along the banks of South Creek. The sites have plenty of room for an RV or a tent, and campsite buffers provide ample privacy for nearly all of the 104 campsites along a narrow loop. A heavily wooded median separates the two main rows of campsites, so no one has to look at anyone else.

Once you camp here, you'll most likely come to request your favorite site again and again. But don't worry about being assigned a site by a ranger, because there isn't a bad site in the campground. For me, it was tough to decide among the many excellent sites that were available during my visit.

Overhead, tall slash pines form the first layer of vegetation. Along South Creek, Spanish moss drapes these and other trees. Beneath the pines grow several smaller types of oak trees and some palms. The oaks twist and turn, stretching for their own piece of sky. The result is ample shade—desirable in this warm place. Thick stands of saw palmetto thrive everywhere, filling in any gaps and making for maximum campsite privacy. The sandy floors of the actual camping areas are the spots not covered with greenery.

Cross South Creek on a wooden bridge and enter the campground. Turn left and pass a row of sixteen campsites lining South Creek. Some of the sites access the creek, but thick undergrowth prevents other campers from having access. A small footbridge crosses the creek past these sites. Then a spur road supports four creekside campsites that are ideal for tent campers.

The sandy main road turns away from the creek, and here begins a row of forty sites all along the outside of the loop. The ground is slightly higher here than along the creek, resulting in slightly less thick vegetation. The dump station and extra car-parking areas are along this row. RV campers prefer these larger, more open sites, and there is still ample shade. Just as the road begins to turn, six pull-through sites cut across. These are designed for the largest RVs.

As the road comes to border South Creek again, more lush sites are found. Tenters seem to favor these smaller sites. Several of these back right against South Creek, which means a great view and easy water access. Campers with pop-ups are also found here. The campground comes to its end beyond these thirty-five sites.

Five fully equipped bathhouses are evenly spread along the median of the narrow loop, so no campers have to walk far to wash up. Four roads cut through the median to minimize campsite drive-throughs. A small playground is located near the first bathhouse.

The busy time here is December through April. Snowbirds in search of warm winter weather keep the campground hopping. But the overall mix is about half tent campers and half RV campers. Be sure to obtain reservations during this time, especially on weekends.

Human and Natural History

One of the species inhabiting Oscar Scherer is the gopher tortoise. This is the only one of the four tortoises of the United States that occurs east of the Mississippi River. The gopher tortoise ranges from south-central Florida to lower Georgia, west to southern Mississippi and a small portion of Louisiana.

This ancient animal prefers well-drained sandy soils and dry habitats like pine flatwoods and sand-pine scrubwoods and coastal dune areas. These are also the habitats that developers like, which puts pressure on the gopher tortoise. Florida now has only a third of its former gopher tortoise population.

The gopher tortoise is best known for digging a burrow that can be forty feet long and ten feet deep. The burrow provides a haven from the heat and cold and from the fires that periodically sweep through tortoise territory. Eventually snakes, mice, rabbits, and many other animals inhabit tortoise burrows, which have evolved into an important component of the overall community—necessary for the survival of many animals.

A tortoise needs nearly as long as a person to mature. The odds of a tortoise egg reaching maturity are slim. After mating, adult female tortoises lay from three to fifteen eggs. Many are eaten by raccoons and other animals. Successful hatchlings live in or near their mother's burrow, but many are eaten at this stage. If the hatchlings survive coyotes, raccoons, and humans, then a tortoise can live more than forty years.

But development is threatening the animal's existence. So are monoculture forestry, hunting tortoises for food, and automobiles. And since the gopher tortoise burrow is so critical to many other life forms in its habitat, if the tortoise is gone, what happens to all the other critters? Protected places like Oscar Scherer State Park provide a natural habitat for the gopher tortoise and all the creatures that it supports.

What To Do

The beaches of Sarasota County are an obvious draw, but before you run off to the sand and surf, check out Oscar Scherer. In addition to several smaller nature trails, the park has developed more than fifteen miles of foot and bicycle trails. There are six trails, designated by color, that traverse through the flatwoods and scrubby pine woods that elsewhere in this part of the state are rapidly disappearing. Of special note is the five-mile White Trail, which loops around the upper stretches of South Creek.

South Creek offers canoeing and fishing. Canoes are for rent at the park. The narrow brooding creek is a great early-morning or late-afternoon paddle. You can fish for snook, redfish, and snapper below the small dam and for freshwater species above it. The freshwater Lake Osprey is just a short walk from the campground and has a small beach of its own, with swimming for anyone at Oscar Scherer who wants to take a dip without taking a drive first.

Surf fishermen and beachcombers need only to head out in either direction along US 41 to access any of the nearby beaches. These public beaches are well maintained by the county and will satisfy your oceanic urges. To reach Nokomis Beach, drive south on US 41 a few miles to Albee Road. Turn right on Albee and you will dead-end at Nokomis. To get to the beaches on Siesta Key, drive north on US 41 and turn left on State Road 72 in Coral Cove. Cross the bridge over to Siesta Key. Turn left on 789 to Turtle Beach and right on 758 to Siesta Key Beach Park. Ask park rangers for directions to any of the other beaches.

What's Nearby

If you tire of the salt water, head inland to Myakka River State Park, one of Florida's oldest preserves. The two freshwater lakes there are known for their birdlife. You can take a nature cruise on the world's largest airboat. The Myakka River is a canoer's delight. It flows through the park for twelve miles. Freshwater fishing is available in both the river and the lakes. Hikers have access to miles and miles of trails that wind through the park's 28,000 acres. Open prairies, small ponds, and pine woods make for a varied terrain.

Located just outside park boundaries are many stores and restaurants. The nearest grocery store is just a few miles south of the park at Nokomis Village Shopping Center. Here also is the Saltwater Cafe, where you can get seafood. Even closer is Rosebuds, where you can choose from a full menu in addition to seafood.

Jonathan Dickinson State Park

If you want to see what southeast Florida looked like 150 years ago, come to Jonathan Dickinson State Park. More than eleven thousand acres support thirteen separate plant communities, including the globally imperiled forested dunes of coastal sand-pine scrub. Campers can also enjoy Florida's only federally designated wild and scenic river, the Loxahatchee, which flows through the park.

Just a few miles away are the numerous beaches of Jupiter Island. These beaches include pristine St. Lucie Inlet and Hobe Sound National Wildlife Refuge as well as many public beaches up and down the lower Treasure Coast.

Two campgrounds in the park offer different habitats to park your rig or pitch your tent. For those who really want to rough it, Jonathan Dickinson also has two backcountry campsites. This former army outpost is now a relaxed operation where your sole mission is to have a good time.

View of Atlantic Ocean from tower atop Hobe Mountain.

☼ ────────────────────────────────

Key Information

Jonathan Dickinson State Park
16450 S.E. Federal Highway
Hobe Sound, FL 33455
(407) 967-2771

Sites: 135

Amenities: Picnic table, fire ring, water spigot, electricity

Registration: By phone or at park entrance booth

Facilities: Hot showers, flush toilets, pay phone, soda machine, pay phone

Fees: $14 per night May–November, $17 per night December–April; $2 electricity

Directions: From Stuart, drive south on US 1 for twelve miles. Jonathan Dickinson State Park will be on your right.

────────────────────────────────

The Beach/Coast

The wild and scenic Loxahatchee River meanders through Jonathan Dickinson. Mangrove lines the river here, but a few miles upstream you'll find an incredible cypress forest and the preserved homestead of the "Wild Man of the Loxahatchee," Trapper Nelson. Downstream the river flows through a state aquatic preserve, exiting into the Atlantic on the south side of Jupiter Island.

The Jupiter Island area is thick with Atlantic beaches. From south to north are Juno Beach Park, Carlin Park, and Jupiter Beach Park. Jupiter Beach is somewhat rocky beneath the water. North of the Loxahatchee are Dubois Park, Blowing Rocks Beach, Hobe Sound Beach, Stuart Beach, and the beach at Hobe Sound National Wildlife Refuge. This 3.5-mile refuge beach is important for green, leatherback, and loggerhead turtle nesting. Thousands of hatchlings emerge from this ecologically significant beach each summer. On the north end of Jupiter Island is St. Lucie Inlet State Preserve. Accessible only in private boats, this pristine beach is also a summer nesting quarters for sea turtles. A boardwalk leads you through nonbeach environments in the park.

From Jonathan Dickinson, Hobe Sound Beach is the most easily accessed. This tawny beach rises sharply from the Atlantic and then levels off, varying in width from fifty to two hundred feet after the rise from the ocean. Stuart Beach is favored by surfers who like the big waves. Most of these public beaches have parking and picnic and bathroom facilities.

The Campground

Two distinctly different camping areas grace this state park (and don't forget the two backcountry sites). The Pine Grove Camping Area is near the park entrance. As the name implies, most of the eighty-five campsites here are located in a grove of nonnative Australian pine. Laid out in a grid beneath the dense tree canopy, nine different "blocks" hold anywhere from seven to sixteen campsites each. A thick duff of pine needles carpets the heavily shaded campsites.

Most of the sites are medium to large with abundant cover and distance between them. This favors RV campers, though some tenters will be seen here as well. The grid layout and two-way paved roads seem confusing at first as you try to find your campsite in the dimness beneath the pines. In the center of the grid is one of two bathhouses; the other is at the south end of the grid.

The River Camping Area is my favorite. It is a few miles from the Pine Grove Camping Area, farther into the heart of the park. The campsites are situated along a loop adjacent to the Loxahatchee River in a mature forest of slash pine. The trunks of these trees head skyward, then branch out high above the tall ground cover of saw palmetto, which park staffers have allowed to grow to maximize camper privacy. Along with patches of sand, luxuriant St. Augustine grass covers the campsite floors.

Most of the forty-three campsites here are on the inside of the loop, which normally means cramped quarters. But this loop is large, and the campsites are generally well separated from one another. In the center of the loop there is a bathhouse surrounded by a green lawn.

If you are a shade lover, stay at Pine Grove. If you like your campsite a little on the sunny side, stay at the River Camping Area. It's not that the sites by the river are completely exposed to the sun; it's just that at some point you will be getting a lot of sun. This loop is generally favored by tent campers, though some RV campers manage to squeeze into the slightly smaller sites.

Jonathan Dickinson is busy from Thanksgiving through Easter. Snowbirds set up camp for extended periods. Weekends during this time are always full. When the weather heats up, the campground becomes empty except on major holidays. Other summer weekends are about half full.

Backpackers have two backcountry campsites from which to choose. Nearly twenty miles of trails wind through the park. The Scrub Jay Campsite is in a drier area of slash pine and has a well for water about a half-mile away. The Kitching Creek Campsite is located on the banks of Kitching Creek and has a well right by the campsite. Get a backcountry permit before you head out on the trail.

Human and Natural History

Jonathan Dickinson didn't really care to see this slice of south Florida that would later be named after him. A Quaker, he and a few of his colleagues were headed Pennsylvania way from Jamaica in 1696 when their boat, Reformation, sank a few miles east of here. They made it to shore and began the arduous trek north to St. Augustine, encountering the Jobe and other Indians. Dickinson recounted his adventures in a journal entitled "God's Protecting Providence."

Another character who came to this place and loved it was Trapper Nelson. In 1936 he headed up the Loxahatchee and established a homesite on the lush riverbank, making a living trapping and selling furs. He built up his homestead and even added a wildlife zoo—maybe to keep him company. It is said that he was quite a loner. He died in 1968, and the state preserved his homesite and grounds.

The coastal sand-pine scrub in the park once covered all of the hilly dunes of southeast Florida. Now it has been all but eliminated by development, making this park all the more important.

The central component of the sand-pine scrub community is the fire-dependent sand pine, which grows on the tall dunes of the park. Several types of oak form an understory along with vines and even the prickly pear cactus, which I'm sure Jonathan Dickinson did not like stepping on.

What To Do

There are a lot of natural options here at Jonathan Dickinson and environs. The first order of business is to climb Hobe Mountain. Hobe Mountain? Yes, it's a 126-foot-high dune located in the sand-pine scrub community that has a tower at its top. Ten minutes from the parking lot will get you a great view of the Atlantic Ocean, Jupiter Island, Hobe Sound, and the unbroken woodland as far to the west as the eye can see. To your south you can make out the tall buildings of south Florida's megalopolis. This view is a real treat in the low-lying Sunshine State.

Now that you have surveyed your domain, start exploring from west to east. Voyaging the Loxahatchee can be done in two ways, by canoe or on the Loxahatchee Queen II. Head upriver and watch the riverbanks change from mangrove to cypress. Tour-boat travelers get a narrated history of the landscape. No matter how you get there, make the stop at Trapper Nelson's and explore the homesite, which is accessible only by water. The river offers salt and freshwater angling. Canoes are for rent at the picnic area if you haven't brought your own.

Land travelers have nearly twenty miles of foot trails to enjoy in the park. The paths wind through every habitat in the park. If you pick only one trail, take the rolling Sand Pine Nature Trail, which starts near the park entrance. Here you can meander among the dunes that harbor this now rare south Florida ecosystem. Bicyclers have their own trail and can also pedal the many miles of paved park roads.

Within just a few miles of the park campgrounds, beach lovers have miles of public beach to enjoy. Load up your vehicle and head out to enjoy the waves, sand, and sun. Or maybe do some surf fishing. Or read a book. Or just feel the breeze blow.

What's Nearby

Ecotourists shouldn't miss the Hobe Sound National Wildlife Refuge. The main office is just across the street from the park. There is a small interpretive museum along Hobe Sound and an adjacent area in sand-pine scrub forest to explore.

Another tract on Jupiter Island houses the remains of old settler homes and a lighthouse built in 1860 that is still in use today. This oceanside tract provides critical beach habitat for oceangoing turtles. Other animals and wading birds need this refuge to maintain their foothold on the territory they once shared with the Jobe Indians.

Near the picnic area is a small store offering limited camp and fishing supplies. The nearest full-service grocery store is a few miles north of the park in the town of Hobe Sound. Two restaurants of note in Hobe Sound are Grumpys and Hobe Sound Pizza. Grumpys is a homespun grill serving reasonably priced eats. Hobe Sound Pizza makes their pies big.

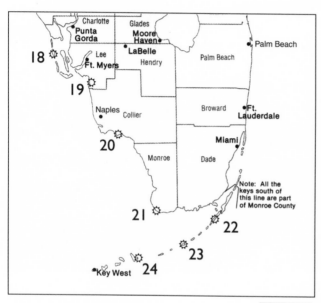

Detail area

18 Cayo Costa State Park

19 Koreshan State Historic Site

20 Collier-Seminole State Park

21 Flamingo

22 John Pennekamp Coral Reef State Park

23 Long Key State Recreation Area

24 Bahia Honda State Park

Oceanfront campsite at Cayo Costa.

Cayo Costa State Park

Have you ever dreamed of escaping to an island where there are no cars, no electricity, and no telephone lines? Leave your vehicle behind and take the ferry to Cayo Costa State Park. This barrier island off the southwest Florida coast meets all the above criteria for escapists and has a few additional features to make your dream world a little more pleasant. How about a thirty-site campground adjacent to a seven-mile stretch of beach? How about some of the best shelling in the state? How about miles of hiking and bicycle trails combing the interior forests of the island? How about south Florida's best beach camping?

Key Information

Barrier Islands GEO Park
P.O. Box 1150
Boca Grande, FL 33921
(941) 964-0375

Sites: 30

Amenities: Picnic table, fire ring

Registration: First come, first served only

Facilities: Cold showers, flush toilets, water spigot

Fees: $13 per night

Directions: From North Fort Myers, take State Road 78 for sixteen miles to Pine Island. Turn right where 78 ends and go four miles to Four Winds Marina, which will be on your left. The *Tropic Star* will boat you out to Cayo Costa.

The goal of the state park service here is to keep Lacosta Island, as Cayo Costa was formerly known, as close to its natural state as possible, re-creating the environment of nearly all barrier islands of five hundred years ago. Since no bridge, telephone, or electric lines were ever installed here, restoring the island to its original state is challenging but not impossible.

That doesn't mean you can't enjoy Cayo Costa now. All it takes is a little preplanning. First, call up the state park, get the telephone number of one of the ferry services, and arrange your transportation to the Cayo Costa from nearby Pine Island. I have enjoyed the service of the *Tropic Star* out of Four Winds Marina on Pine Island. Their number is (941) 283-0015. If you have your own boat, then you are already set. Bring all the food, gear, and supplies that you can anticipate you'll need. Then bring a little more. The only thing you can purchase on the island is ice, so load your cooler. Get to your ferry on time, hop aboard, and say good-bye to the cruel world as it sinks beyond the horizon.

The Beach/Coast

Cayo Costa is part of the so-called Barrier Islands GEO Park, which includes several islands in the area. Cayo Costa itself is seven miles long and about a mile wide at its widest point. Your first view of the island will be your approach from Pelican Bay as you swing around Punta Blanca Island. Mangrove grows right to the water on most of this side of the island, which is punctuated with small inlets and some narrow beach areas. Other small islands dot the horizon as you look back toward the mainland.

The north tip of Cayo Costa looks over Gasparrilla Island, Boca Grande Pass, and the village of Boca Grande. This is known as Quarantine Point. Then you round the island to the Gulf side. The beach gradually becomes wider. Beyond you is nothing but ocean all the way to the horizon. Okay, maybe a boat or two may be passing by. Anyway, here begins the beachcomber's paradise. Small shells pile up along the high-tide line. There are no cars or construction noises, just the serenade of the surf. A sand-scrub environment ekes out a living just in from the beach. Farther south the island narrows. The beach stretches on for miles; the farther south you walk the more isolated the beach and the better the shelling becomes.

Arrive at the south tip of the island and look over Captiva Pass and North Captiva Island. Once again, the side facing Pine Island and the mainland is dominated by mangrove. Keep heading farther north and you find yourself back at the bay side dock and Pelican Bay.

The Campground

Riding the ferry is just the first step in getting to the campground. Unload your gear off the ferry and register at the campground office. Then load your gear onto the park tram, which will take you about a mile to the Gulf side of the island. You may ride in a cart behind a tractor or on an old school bus. Either way the ride will be slow and easy, in the laid-back Cayo Costa style, over an old shell road.

Disembark in front of the campground and unload your gear. Leave your stuff right there for a minute and pick out a campsite or you'll be hauling your things all over the campground. This campground is undergoing some serious changes. There may or may not be Australian pines by the time you get there. These trees provide good shade but are nonnative and are going to be removed and replaced with native sea grape and strangler fig trees.

The first eight campsites are in a cleared area facing the beach. Three of the campsites look over the beach, with some small sea grape trees to cut the breeze. Two campsites are beside the tram drop-off, and the rest are dispersed farther back from the ocean and set into some more mature sea grape. There is little under-story between these campsites. Some sites are low-lying and prone to flooding during a storm. Keep that in mind.

Another row of five campsites is strung along facing the beach. The first three sites are very close together, affording little privacy but offering a great ocean view. The last two campsites are open to the ocean and backed on three sides by sea grape. This arrange-ment avails privacy but is very sunny during the midday hours. These are the two most desirable campsites.

Behind the first row of campsites is a second row of eleven sites. A few palm trees are mixed in with the thick growth of sea grapes that separates the two rows of campsites. Some of the sites are lit-erally under a low canopy of vegetation, providing an almost cavelike setting. This row is desirable during times of high wind or cold weather, but can be buggy.

The final camping area has eight sites amid sea grape, palm, strangler fig, and some saw palmetto. These campsites are farthest from the beach, and are the newest. They are integrated into the restored native environment. Three of the campsites run straight-away from the beach and are so nestled into the vegetation they are almost hard to find.

Three small bathhouses serve the campground and the adjacent cabins. Two bathhouses are closer to the cabins and one is next to the campground. There are flush toilets for men and women and cold-water outdoor showers. The park asks you not to use soap while showering as there is no system to remove the soap. Sinks and spigots with potable water are also located at these bath-houses.

Cayo Costa is fairly busy from Thanksgiving until Easter, but you can almost always get a campsite. There are no reservations; it's first come, first served. Cayo Costa dies down during the summer months except for the major holidays. This is the only time, along with tarpon fishing tournaments, that the campground is guaranteed to be full. Plan accordingly.

Human and Natural History

Cayo Costa was originally part of the far-flung empire of the Calusa Indians, who occupied many of the barrier islands of the southwest Florida coast. The island was later settled by Cuban fishermen, who would stop there to salt and dry their fish and sail on to Cuba. Eventually some Cubans stayed year-round, building cabbage palm houses on the north end of the island and establishing permanent fishing operations and even a school here.

Later, the United States saw Cayo Costa as a potential military base to protect the deep Boca Grande Pass, the only entrance into Charlotte harbor. It took thirty-three years to move the settlers, who migrated to the central and south parts of the island, continuing their way of life until 1958.

The north end of the island eventually became a county park, with the state taking care of the south end. In 1983 the state took over the entire operation. There are some private inholdings on Cayo Costa that are slated to be purchased by the state.

Cayo Costa is being restored to its natural state. This means the elimination of Brazilian pepper, also known as the Florida holly, and of Australian pine, which provides much shade. As they eliminate the persistent pines and peppers, park personnel are trying to regrow native species to provide shade. Years from now, Cayo Costa will look very much like all barrier islands a half millennium ago.

What To Do

While visiting with a fellow camper at Cayo Costa I asked the question, "What is on your agenda today?" She replied, "That's why I came here, so I wouldn't have an agenda." That about sums this place up. Cayo Costa is about relaxing and leaving the stresses of work and home life behind. It's a vacation, a respite, an escape. It's when you gauge time by the movement of the sun and make your next move when you get the whim. It's time to let your mind wander or to get lost in that book you've been meaning to read.

And when you are good and ready there's plenty else to do. Nearly everyone who comes here goes shelling. Because there is no auto access, there are some great shells to be had for those who make the effort to get here. Here's a tip for shellers: the farther south you head from the campground, the more interesting shells you are apt to find. Of course, many just like to walk the beach and listen to the waves and watch the birds and feel the wind blow.

Hikers and bikers can enjoy the many miles of trails that crisscross the island. You can see an old island cemetery and get a view from Quarantine Point and hike along the Gulf. I had a ball biking around the island.

What's Nearby

Since Cayo Costa is a barrier island with no road access, your options outside the park are extremely limited. However, many of the ferry services take visitors to nearby Cabbage Key, which is visible from the bayside dock. There is a restaurant and bar on Cabbage Key. This is purportedly the restaurant where Jimmy Buffet, then an unknown singer, was inspired to write the song "Cheeseburger In Paradise." Beyond Cabbage Key, it's up to you to make your own paradise on Cayo Costa.

Koreshan State Historic Site

A man comes to Florida with a vision of a new community based on a religion he started after having an "illumination." Question: What does this have to do with beach and coastal camping in Florida? Answer: The location of this man's "New Jerusalem" on the alluring Estero River is now owned by the state of Florida and makes for a fine base camp for exploring the rivers, beaches, and solemn swamps of the southwest coast.

Back to the story. Dr. Cyrus Teed, who renamed himself Koresh after his illumination experience, founded a new version of Christianity based on communal living, celibacy, a universe inside the earth, and his own immortality. The idea of a universe inside the

Bamboo Landing on the Estero River.

Key Information

Koreshan State Historic Site
P.O. Box 7
Estero, FL 33928
(941) 992-0311

Sites: 60

Amenities: Picnic table, fire ring, water spigot, electricity

Registration: By phone or at park entrance booth

Facilities: Hot showers, flush toilets, pay phone, laundry

Fees: $10 per night May–November, $16 per night December–April, $2 electricity

Directions: From Fort Myers, head south on US 41 for one mile to the intersection with Corkscrew Road. Turn right on Corkscrew Road and follow it just a few yards. Koreshan State Historic Site will be on your right.

earth was called "cellular cosmogony," which Teed "discovered" in 1870. Some people believed him and followed him to the remote Estero River in 1894 to form a community, where they practiced what Teed preached until he died. After his lack of immortality was exposed, the sect began to dwindle, and in 1961 the remaining members donated the communal land to the state in Teed's memory.

So now we have a historic park with an attractively wooded riverside campground in the middle of the fast-growing Fort Myers area. What once was the back of beyond for Teed and his followers has become a refuge from development in Lee County. The campsites here offer above-average scenery for tent and RV campers alike. Lovers Key and Bonita Beach are just a few miles away. Nearby Corkscrew Swamp Sanctuary, owned by the Audubon Society, is a natural world of its own. Mound Key State Archaeological Site features evidence of two thousand years of human occupation and is just a canoe ride away from the campground boat launch.

The existence of the Koreshan State Historic Site demonstrates that the demise of a cult isn't always an unhappy ending.

The Beach/Coast

One look at the Estero River will show you why Florida saw fit to designate it a state canoe trail. Palm trees and live oaks draped in Spanish moss extend along the banks of the transparent tea-colored water. Ferns and sawgrass line the watercourse; in other places slash pines tower above the limestone and sand edges of the river. The Estero steadily widens on its course to Estero Bay, where Mound Key and other islands form a barrier in the Gulf of Mexico. A good mile of river sweeps around the historic buildings and the campground of the park. A nature trail runs along much of the stream. Bamboo Landing, part of the Koreshan settlement, is just one of many river-access points in the park itself, including a palm-studded picnic area. Fishermen and birdwatchers laze the day away near the boat launch. The word "Estero" is Spanish for "estuary." This lush environment is very deserving of the name.

In the area are numerous beaches. From north to south you start with Sanibel Beach, a sheller's paradise on Sanibel Island. Then comes Fort Myers Beach and state-owned Lovers Key. Farther south are Bonita Beach, Barefoot Beach, and finally Delnor-Wiggins Pass State Recreation Area, which also draws shellers. All of these beaches are within a half-hour drive of Koreshan.

The Campground

The campground is ingeniously designed along four one-way roads that minimize traffic and maximize campsite privacy. Nearly all the campsites are well buffered from one another and look across the road at the natural landscape instead of other campers. Twisted scrub oaks, stately palms, and towering slash pines dominate the scenery. Saw palmetto and thick brush thrive in the understory, creating a natural tangle of vegetation that gives each camp group its own little paradise. Limestone rocks, unearthed when water and electrical lines were laid, add an unusual aesthetic touch. The groundcover is primarily sand with some grass.

An initial one-way road has no campsites along it. This cuts down on campsite drivebys. The first row of thirteen sites comes in on the left. These are the largest and most open sites in the campground. The oaks are smaller here, and the palms are fewer, but the campsite buffers are thick as ever. RV campers and sun lovers will choose these sites. The second row is a thick mixture of sabal palm and oak that looks across a median of natural woods. This row contains fifteen campsites of varying sizes. Choose your site according to the size of your rig.

The third row contains nineteen smaller sites that are extensively sheltered beneath a canopy of pine and oak. Some sites are in lower areas that could be prone to flooding. Some of the sites are deep enough to fit an RV, while others are tent-only. The adequate understory allows you to move about your camp without wondering if your neighbor is watching your every move.

As evidenced by the last row of campsites, as you get closer to the river, palm trees become more prevalent. The last row, with eleven campsites that are the park's best, runs parallel to the river, whereas the other rows run perpendicular. The sites are short and wide and enjoy a great deal of shade provided by a plethora of sabal palms. Informal paths lead right down to the Estero River.

This is where tent campers will want to stay.

In the middle of the whole sixty-site affair is a fine bathhouse with hot showers, a laundry facility, a soda machine, and a pay phone. Paths are cut into the brush to allow campers to access the bathhouse from all directions without cutting through other campers' temporary homes.

Koreshan is a winter destination. Snowbirds escaping the cold of the north country will stay their full two weeks. And area growth brings other visitors. Between Christmas and the end of April, whether on a weekday or the weekend, it is wise to make a reservation.

After April the campground at Koreshan resembles the ghost town that is the historic settlement. Weekends see a few water enthusiasts. The mosquitoes become a little more pesky but aren't that bad. It's the heat that drives most campers into air-conditioning.

Human and Natural History

Each member of the Koreshan sect was to work for the good of all. Both traditional and vocational education were stressed, as was Koreshan cosmogony and how the world worked according to Koresh. Members were offered a secure, insulated life, a "New Jerusalem" that Koresh said would eventually expand to millions of people in a planned city. What you see today, the Home Grounds, is about as big as it got. There were some nearby offshoots in places such as Mound Key. But to turn wilderness into settlement is a lot of hard work, and people weren't easily converted to the task. Consequently we can assume that the development of the planned community lagged due to a labor shortage.

The group was self-sufficient, selling excess goods, including bread and some finished goods, to outsiders. They continued working on their community until Teed died. Members refused to bury their leader, thinking he would rise from the dead, until the Lee County coroner forced them to reconsider. He was placed in a tomb, which was destroyed in a 1921 hurricane. His body was never recovered.

Without Teed, recruiting new Koreshans was difficult, and the celibacy policy of the cult got in the way of reproducing new members. As the group aged, the Koreshans saw the end. The last Koreshan to live at the settlement, Mrs. Hedwig Michel, is buried on the grounds.

Nearby Corkscrew Swamp Sanctuary is in the wild and pristine state in which Teed found much of southwest Florida. The National Audubon Society saw fit to purchase and protect the five-hundred-year-old bald cypress trees and accompanying ecosystem, where tropical flowers bloom and wildlife thrives in a natural setting unfettered by the Sunshine State land boom.

The longest-running-history award goes to Mound Key. Around the time of the birth of Christ, Mound Key was barely above water, but ancestors of the Calusa Indians began to harvest the rich waters of Estero Bay, piling their shells and remains on the island and literally raising its height. The Calusa sculpted the shell mounds, forming canals and water courts. Mound Key is believed to have been the Calusa capital when the Spanish arrived. The remains of their culture can be seen today.

What To Do

The first order of business is a tour of the Koreshan Unity Historic District. A booklet will aid you. Ranger-led tours are offered on weekends. Look inside the restored buildings and read the displays to gain insight on a religious commune of days gone by. The gardens demonstrate the sect's appreciation of form and order. The machine shop and bakery show a more practical side of the Koreshans, who wanted to make life on the home ground both efficient and profitable. The Art Hall was the cultural and religious center of Koreshan life. Look at the stage, the paintings, and other relics of an eccentric religion.

After your history lesson, check out the natural beauty of the park. The Estero River is the centerpiece. Canoes are offered for rent at the boat ramp, where you can also launch your own craft. Walkers can stroll the riverside nature trail, which offers scenes of the dark, shady, tide-influenced Estero. Upstream of the landing you may catch a bass. Downstream you'll encounter strictly salt-water species.

Make time to visit Mound Key. It's a two-hour paddle from the launch out to the island, but it is very much worth it. Once you're out there, you can take a shell path that traverses the island over two mounds that are the highest "natural" points in Lee County. If you stumble onto an artifact, however, please leave it alone, for archaeologists are still piecing together the puzzle of human habitation on Mound Key.

With so many beaches nearby, it's hard to choose just one. Bonita Beach is less crowded than others. Lovers Key is state-run, so it's better preserved in its natural condition. Fishing, hiking, and swimming are available. Sanibel Beach and Delnor-Wiggins Pass offer the best shelling opportunities. Sanibel Beach also has a lighthouse nearby.

Any time of the year is a good time to visit Corkscrew Swamp. A two-mile boardwalk makes for a dry-footed trip through the pristine forest east of Koreshan.

What's Nearby

Civilization has made it out to the site where Teed's vision came into being. Once Estero was a slow-moving, sun-drenched village. Now development has moved up from Naples and down from Fort Myers, nearly connecting in the center. For sure, while you're at Koreshan you'll have access to wide variety of restaurant and supply opportunities just a short drive away. Eventually, Koreshan will be surrounded. The Estero River forms a beautiful natural barrier. So look at Koreshan as an escape from the bustle of the Tamiami Trail.

Collier-Seminole State Park

Collier-Seminole occupies the northern fringe of the Ten Thousand Islands and is a mini-Everglades on the coast of Southwest Florida. Here you'll find tropical hammock woodland like that which occurs in few other places in the state. The rare royal palm is a common species here. Nearby Marco Island has Tigertail Beach, and the Fakahatchee Strand south of Collier-Seminole is one of the most important preserved natural habitats left in the state.

There is much to see and do at Collier-Seminole. Just make sure to plan to visit between December and April, when the weather is drier and cooler. That means fewer mosquitoes—this can be one of the buggiest parks in the state. The bugs take over in summer, with hardly a human in sight, except for the park rangers.

Both RVers and tent campers can enjoy the attractive yet sizable campground. More adventurous campers have two self-propelled options: by foot in the woodlands or by canoe in the park wilderness preserve. The preserve is a mangrove swamp bridging the

Entrance to the park.

─ ☼ ─

Key Information

Collier-Seminole State Park
20200 East Tamiami Trail
Naples, FL 33961
(941) 394-3397

Sites: 81 water and electricity, 46 water only

Amenities: Picnic table, fire ring, water spigot

Registration: By phone or at park entrance booth

Facilities: Hot showers, flush toilets, pay phone, laundry, dump
station

Fees: $8 per night May–November, $13 per night December–April,
$2 electricity

Directions: From Naples head south on US 41 for fifteen miles.
Collier-Seminole State Park will be on your right.

Gulf and the sawgrass. The backcountry hiking option traverses
pine flatlands and other environments endemic to southwest
Florida.

Heed the bug warning, but don't pass this place by. It is always a
rewarding leg in my south Florida runs. Be glad there is a set-
aside chunk of real estate in this rapidly developing part of the
state. You can thank Barron Collier, an early developer who had a
large stake in building the east-west coast connector now known
as the Tamiami Trail, for having the foresight to preserve some of
his holdings. More about the Tamiami Trail later.

The Beach/Coast

The park proper preserves the northwestern edge of the Everglades. The area is primarily mangrove forest, part of the largest
contiguous mangrove forest in the world. Whether mangrove ar-

eas are actually land is up for consideration. Propped up by arched roots extending into mostly brackish water, mangroves grow in dense thickets that form what look like islands. Mud and decayed vegetation form a muck that is exposed with the rise and fall of the tides. These mangrove thickets are dissected by channels that transport the freshwater flowing out of the sawgrass of the Glades to the ocean. Tides move water in and out of these channels, where fish thrive and birds make their homes. Manatees and alligators also call these waters home.

This area is also the northern terminus of the famous Ten Thousand Islands. The mangroves form a confusing maze of islands called "keys." The area adjacent to Collier-Seminole forms part of the Cape Romano–Ten Thousand Islands Aquatic Preserve. Boaters can easily become confused while touring the Gulf scenery or fishing the rich waters, which are also home to stone crabs. Stone-crab harvesting is a primary occupation for many residents of nearby Everglades City.

Marco Island, just north of Collier-Seminole, is home to Tigertail Beach. It has several public-access points and faces out into the Gulf of Mexico. It is a great place to watch the sun set.

The Campground

Collier-Seminole offers an excellent campground that exudes a tropical feel. Royal palms sway overhead. Live oaks and pine form additional understory. This is the most tropical-looking campground in the state. Normally a campground with 130 sites can seem like a tent city, but the layout here spreads the sites far enough apart to minimize the crowding effect.

The first nineteen campsites are on an oval loop of their own. Six of these sites are on the inside of the loop. They have water and electricity and are cut into a thick tropical forest. Each campsite is secluded from its neighbors by saw palmetto, ferns, brush, scrub live oaks, and palms. The brush makes the sites narrow, most appropriate for tent campers. RVers occasionally will make the tight squeeze into one of these sites. Privacy comes with a price, however; the dense vegetation cuts down on breezes, making for a potentially hotter and buggier experience. A short path leads to a fully equipped comfort station with hot showers.

The second loop has an unusual triangle configuration with crushed-shell roads cutting across the triangle. The understory is virtually nonexistent here, but the grassy lawn is a good place to set out your folding chair. Palms, oaks, and pines are attractively interspersed throughout the triangle, providing adequate shade. Fifty-three of the 110 campsites are on the outside of the triangle, and all have water and electricity. RVers will feel comfortable pulling in and out of these campsites onto crushed-shell pads from the paved road.

The inner part of the triangle has water-only sites, with the exception of ten water and electricity sites in one inside corner. All of the sites are generally spacious enough for RVers or tent campers who want to park their vehicles and spread out their gear. You may even see an occasional boat on a trailer. The center of the triangle has a fully equipped bathhouse. At the front of the triangle is another smaller bathhouse attached to a screened-in meeting room. Here campers gather for coffee in the morning and cards in the evening. It's a great place to meet your neighbors. During inclement weather, interpretive programs are presented in the meeting room.

Collier-Seminole is busy from after Christmas through April. Snowbirds from the North will stay here for the maximum-allotted two weeks, then move on. Get a reservation on weekends. You can usually slip in on weekdays. After April until the fall cooldown, you'll find only the mosquitoes, the rangers, and a few hardy souls with a masochistic vein.

The same is true for the backcountry adventurers. Backpackers can take the park hiking trail to a campsite in an oak and palm hammock. But you must bring your own water. Campfires are allowed. Canoers paddling to the Grocery Place campsite, a smidgen of land enclosed by mangrove, must bring their own supplies, but they'll be rewarded with the solitude of the Everglades.

Human and Natural History

Barron Collier was the primary force in the construction of the Tamiami Trail, which runs right by Collier-Seminole. Extending from Tampa to Miami, hence the name, the Tamiami absorbed more than a million of Collier's dollars, a huge investment when he made it in the 1920s. One of the reasons he considered it a fairly safe bet was the walking dredge, an odd-looking yet important piece of machinery that was used to turn the cypress swamps and wooded hammocks into useable road. It is now on display at Collier-Seminole.

Built in Michigan, the dredge was used to dig a canal, which provided rock fill for the roadbed and drainage for the completed road. It could walk over rough, swampy ground and among close-cut stumps. The walking dredge could cover eighty feet in a ten-hour shift.

But first the land had to be cleared of trees and brush. Then holes were drilled into the limestone beneath the swamps. Dynamite was placed in the holes, breaking up the rock into pieces small enough for the dredge to handle. More than 2.5 million sticks of dynamite were exploded during the project.

Life was rough for the dredge operators and other workers. They lived along with their families in portable bunkhouses, following the road. Small fans made from saw palmetto were used to swat away the clouds of bugs. Working in ever-present water caused a variety of foot ailments. Worker salaries ranged from $75 to $150 per month. And you thought you had it rough!

A scant twelve miles south of the park, the Fakahatchee Strand State Preserve protects an elongated swamp forest running along a channel that forms the southwestern edge of the Big Cypress Swamp. These islandlike forests are called "strands" because they are long and narrow and stand out from the horizon of sawgrass around them.

This strand, twenty miles long by five miles wide, is almost entirely protected by the state. The water that flows through here is vital to the Everglades ecosystem. The Florida panther and the black bear roam the strand amid rare tropical species such as the royal palm and the largest concentration of orchids in North America.

What To Do

Collier-Seminole is a nature lover's park. Most park enthusiasts don't leave until they have explored the wilderness preserve. More than four thousand acres of salt marsh, mangrove, and sea are just a boat ride away. Canoes are for rent at the park near Boat Basin, where there is a boat launch for your own hand- or motor-powered craft. A marked 13.5-mile canoe trail, one of only thirty-six designated state canoe trails, makes a loop through the preserve. Camping is permitted at Grocery Place. Bring your bug repellent no matter what the time of year. The fishing is saltwater and I can say first hand that the fish are there. You may land snook, reds, mangrove snapper, or Jack Crevalle.

Park-sponsored boat tours, guided by a local who gives a pretty fair narrative on the history of the area, take you through the mangrove. The tours leave Boat Basin every ninety minutes.

On the other side of US 41 is a 6.5-mile-long hiking trail that will lead you through everything from grassy plains to junglesque woods with plenty of wildlife. I saw an owl carrying a snake off in its talons. Expect to get your feet wet somewhere along the way. Staying overnight at the backcountry campsite adds a dimension to the Collier-Seminole hiking experience. The Royal Palm Nature Trail is a much shorter day-hiking trail. It starts near the Boat Basin and explores a wood reminiscent of the Caribbean.

It is said that the Fakahatchee Strand may be the most valuable slice of natural Florida in the state, so many are the rare plant and animal species there. Take the boardwalk and explore the habitat of which they are part. Head south on US 41 for twelve miles. The strand will be on your left.

Sun worshipers can make the pilgrimage to Marco Island. Turn left out of the park and turn left again on State Road 92. Tigertail Beach is on the northern end of the island. Public access is plentiful. There is a small parking fee.

What's Nearby

The vastness of Everglades National Park is just south of Collier-Seminole. There is a visitor center in Everglades City. Another large component of the south Florida landscape is the Big Cypress National Preserve. Together, these federal lands comprise a few million acres and would require a lifetime to explore.

For quick supply runs there is a park store at Boat Basin and a convenience store just north of the park. The nearest full-service grocery store is ten miles north on US 41. Dining options include the Crazy Flamingo on Marco Island, which offers food and fun. For the local delicacy, stone crab, or for any other seafood, head to the Grouper House. It is north on 41, as are most other food and supply options.

Flamingo

Flamingo campground occupies the most southerly parcel of terra firma on the Florida mainland. Farther south is island-studded Florida Bay. To the north is the largest roadless area in the United States—it's known as the Everglades. Flamingo is campers' headquarters for all those who wish to explore one of America's finest natural resources, Everglades National Park.

From these headquarters you can see what the Everglades really are: a vast ecosystem powered by water that moves from the plains of sawgrass through the richest stands of mangrove on the planet, to pristine, undeveloped beaches astride the Gulf, to scores of remote ocean islands, all protected by national park status. You'll never want to leave this former fishing village at the end of

Two friends enjoy a sunset at Cape Sable.

☼

Key Information

Everglades National Park
40001 State Road
Homestead, FL 33034
(305) 242-7700

Sites: 288

Amenities: Picnic table, stand-up grill

Registration: By phone or at park entrance booth

Facilities: Water spigot, cold showers, flush toilets, pay phone

Fees: $14 per night

Directions: From US 1 in Florida City, follow the signs south to Everglades National Park. Flamingo Campground is thirty-eight miles beyond the park entrance gate on the main campground road.

---

a two-lane road. Once the spell of the Glades has been cast, most likely you'll come back for more. Over the past decade I've spent at least a week down here every year since I first laid eyes on the place.

The Beach/Coast

The Everglades covers far more coastline than any other park covered in this book. Starting just south of the Miami metroplex, the park encompasses the small islands of Florida Bay and the mangrove shorelines east of Flamingo, where crocodiles thrive. Closer to Flamingo are points of land that jut into Florida Bay and a coastal prairie that offers vistas of the ocean.

Around Flamingo is a full-scale marina where boats of all sizes and descriptions come and go. Then begins Cape Sable, aptly described as one of the finest pieces of real estate in North America. A series of beaches stretches west and then north, encompassing the southwest tip of the state. The Coastal Prairie Trail extends along the southerly tip of the cape. Backcountry campsites for boaters occupy selected points along the cape. I've simply never seen a finer sunset in the world than from Cape Sable.

North of Cape Sable you'll find alternating stretches of beach and mangrove coastline accessible only by boat. Highland Beach is my favorite spot here. It's a steep beach rising right out of the ocean, where you can spend a lazy day just watching ships pass in the distance.

Farther up from Highland Beach you'll see the beginning of the famous Ten Thousand Islands. Here a myriad of small mangrove islands form a coastal maze extending for miles up the coast, beyond Everglades City and the formal boundaries of the national park. Some of these keys have small beaches, and all exude a sense of wild remoteness that cannot be experienced on any other coast in the lower forty-eight.

The Campground

By the 1990s it had become apparent that Flamingo's infrastructure, built in 1959, was crumbling. The campground facilities have received a recent overhaul. The natural setting was always more than adequate.

Flamingo has two campgrounds right on Florida Bay. One campground is for tenters only, and the other is for tent, pop-up, and RV campers. Both have new bathrooms with flush toilets and cold-water showers. The atmosphere here is laid back. Everything moves at the pace of the sun across the sky, like a former fishing village should.

The tent and RV campground is made up of four loops. Each loop is an oval with side roads cutting across it like rows in a movie theater. Each of these side roads houses from five to ten campsites, which lie beneath landscaped native trees such as buttonwood, gumbo limbo, and palm. These tropical trees add to the seaside atmosphere. Each of the loops has two bathhouses. There are no water or electrical hookups. You must get your water from spigots located by the bathhouses.

As business increases, park personnel open another loop. So A loop fills, then B loop is opened. Then C loop, furthest back from the campground entrance, follows. The fourth loop, T loop, is on a spur road of its own. It is reserved for those big RVs that prefer a pull-through site. So if you are driving a big rig, bring her on down to Flamingo because there are plenty of spots waiting for you.

If your rig is a nylon tent, come on down to the walk-in tent-camping area. It is the more scenic of the two camping loops. The sixty-four campsites here are situated in a grassy field abutting Florida Bay. Palm trees and a few other shade trees dot the grassy area, but there is far more sun than shade. The grassy field extends all the way to the water, with the exception of one stretch where shoreline trees obscure an otherwise fantastic view of all the keys in Florida Bay.

Park your car in the common parking area and tote your stuff a short distance to your tent campsite. Each campsite is designated with a numbered stand-up grill. All campsites have a picnic table. Two bathhouses serve the seemingly randomly laid-out sites of the tent campground. The setting is scenic, but the lack of shade can be bothersome on a hot day. The breezy openness of the campground can be a plus on buggy days.

The bugs and heat all but close the place by May. After May camping is free, but there are no facilities and only an occasional camper who is willing to be eaten alive while sweltering in the sun. The winter months can be fantastic, with warm days and cool nights. In winter, mosquitoes are certainly less of a problem than in summer. With nearly three hundred campsites, the park is so large that reservations are rarely necessary, but you may wish to call ahead for peace of mind.

Human and Natural History

Everglades National Park contains less than half of the entire Everglades ecosystem. From the huge Kissimmee River basin, fresh water moves in a thin, miles-wide sheet southward through the sawgrass. In this sawgrass are islands of higher ground, where tropical trees grow in "hammocks," forming mini-ecosystems where deer and the reclusive panthers reside.

As the water spreads south, it meets the salt water of the ocean, which presses inland with the ebb and flow of the tides. Here mangrove stands rise from the rich waters. Dolphins and sharks swim alongside gamefish such as snook and reds. Smaller fish are fare for the incredible variety of birds, including osprey and several varieties of heron.

Finally, the brackish water enters the Gulf of Mexico, Florida Bay, and the Ten Thousand Islands area. The southeastern Everglades is the only American home of the crocodile. The Everglades is the only place in the world where the alligator and the crocodile reside side by side. But this is just one unique aspect of the unique ecosystem that is the Everglades. That is why the park is designated a World Heritage Site.

The birds of the park once were hunted for their feathers, and they have never recovered to their original numbers. Still, such creatures as the roseate spoonbill make for a colorful sight when you do spot them. Unfortunately, the park is always under the gun. Water is diverted to nearby Miami, and pesticide runoff from agriculture pollutes what remains, and exotic fish and plants have invaded and caused much disruption. The system of the Everglades is based on the seasonal flow of water, and the alteration of that flow has changed everything. Park managers are trying to cope with this conflict between the demands of Miami and the rest of the urban east coast and the needs of the plants and animals of the Everglades.

What To Do

From Flamingo campground you can enjoy the southern side of the park, which harbors many different environments. As you drive into the park, make your first stop the new visitor center. The museum displays explain the web of life that is the Everglades. Beyond the visitor center are the Pinelands. Hikers can enjoy the miles of trails that course through some of the Glades' driest land. Get a view of the river of grass from Pa-hay-okee Overlook. A must stop is the Mahogany Hammock. Here you make a loop on an elevated boardwalk through a tropical hardwood hammock. It's a whole new world. This is my favorite Everglades trail.

Next, head to Flamingo and set up camp. Coast lovers will want to walk the Guy Bradley Trail, which leaves from the Flamingo Visitor Center. Catch a south Florida sunset, then plan your activities for the next day. You can use your feet, a canoe, a motorboat, a sailboat, a tour boat, or an auto to explore the landscape. A park-authorized concessionaire operates rentals in case you leave your own craft at home. I urge you to bring your own craft if possible, however, for the rental fees are mighty steep. The concessionaire has the local market cornered.

In the immediate campground area you'll find other hiking trails. There is an informative handout of both hiking and canoe trails that will help you pick the right path for you. Some trails allow bikes. Bikers will also be found tooling along the main park roads, which are fairly quiet. The Eco Pond Loop is known particularly for its birdwatching opportunities.

Because this is such a watery place, it stands to reason that you need to get out on the water to really see what's going on. A quiet canoe trip will sometimes reap large rewards for ecotourists. The Nine Mile Pond Trail actually travels only five miles but can be a boon for birders. Since motors are not allowed, you can get back to communing with the "real world." I do not recommend the Hells Bay Trail. Too many twists and turns can frustrate the novice canoeist. Consult the park handout for other options. Fishermen can work a pole into their watery plans.

You can also take a cruise into the backcountry, or into Florida Bay, or into Whitewater Bay—or you can just sail off into the sunset. Contact the concessionaire for departure times and prices for these sightseeing cruises. There is more here to do than the average camper has time for.

What's Nearby

The Flamingo experience at Everglades National Park is an all-inclusive endeavor. There is plenty to see and do in this vast preserve. Before you enter the park, collect all the supplies you think you will need. However, there is a marina store that charges really high prices for limited supplies. Just try to limit your purchases to ice and souvenirs and you'll be fine.

For your dining pleasure there are two restaurants near the Flamingo Visitor Center. The Buttonwood Patio is a more casual affair, offering burgers and such in an outdoor setting overlooking Florida Bay. I have enjoyed a few post-canoeing meals and cold beverages there. Upstairs is the Flamingo Restaurant, offering breakfast, lunch, and dinner. Specialties naturally involve seafood. What else would you expect from an area that was once a fishing village?

John Pennekamp Coral Reef State Park

John Pennekamp holds the distinction of being America's first undersea park. Before you imagine an underwater campground, understand that a section of developed shoreline goes along with the 178 nautical miles of coral reefs and other ocean environments, sheltered beneath clear warm waters that are ideal for snorkeling and scuba diving. More than six hundred species of fish, crabs, and lobsters make their home among the coral reefs.

This busy park has an average campground to go along with multiple facilities intended to further your enjoyment of the reefs. Inside the park, concessionaires operate glass-bottomed boats, snorkeling services, and sailing and diving operations. There is also some above-water "real Florida" to enjoy, including two

Early morning at Far Beach.

Key Information

John Pennekamp Coral Reef State Park
Post Office Box 487
Key Largo, FL 33037
(305) 451-1202

Sites: 47

Amenities: Picnic table, fire ring, water spigot, electricity

Registration: By phone or at park entrance booth

Facilities: Hot showers, flush toilets, pay phone

Fees: $22 per night, $2 electricity

Directions: John Pennekamp Coral Reef State Park is south of Miami
at mile marker 102.5 of US 1 on Key Largo. The park will be on your
left.

beaches, two hiking trails, and a thirty-thousand-gallon living
aquarium at the visitors center.

Just about everybody at John Pennekamp ends up in or on the
water in one way or another. Many fishermen and divers embark
from the park's marina, while others canoe and kayak. Still others
rent sea cycles, bumper boats, and small sailboats. This is an active
camper's park; nearly everyone is doing something. So if you have
come to watch the breeze blow, look out, because someone is
gonna knock you down on their way to the water!

The Beach/Coast

The land portion of John Pennekamp is situated on Key Largo at the southwestern edge of Largo Sound. Largo Sound forms a bay between Key Largo and Radabob Key, a mangrove island that lies between the state park and the Atlantic Ocean. Two channels lead north and south out of Largo Sound to the Atlantic. Interesting undersea life thrives in Largo Sound and beyond into the Atlantic.

In the developed area of John Pennekamp the mangrove gives way first to Cannon Beach, a popular swimming and snorkeling area. Here palm trees and sea grape give some seaside shade near actual mounted cannons on the sand. The sand leads down to a roped-off swim area with a floating pier that also harbors a replica of a Spanish shipwreck below the translucent blue ocean.

Beyond Cannon Beach is the main marina area. Slips for private boats and a boat ramp are here. Across the bridge from the marina is a mangrove and sand island where another swim area is located. Swimmers and snorkelers interact with the water and the life within it.

Also on this island is a boardwalk that cuts through a mangrove thicket and follows a tidal creek. At the end of this area is Far Beach. This is the most popular beach for sunbathers. A shaded picnic shelter and palm trees are found next to a clear pool of ocean water. A circular rock partition divides the swimming area from the rest of Largo Sound. Other small creeks and channels wind through the mangrove nearby.

The Campground

The campground doesn't begin to match the underwater or above-ground facilities at John Pennekamp—it's the weak link of the park. It may only be that the rest of the park sets too-high standards, but the campground is so busy year-round that it can barely maintain itself under the stress of daily use. I'm not saying that you shouldn't camp here; just don't make camping an end in itself. Camp here to give yourself instant access to the rest of John Pennekamp.

The campground lies along a wide, two-way gravel road that spurs off the marina parking lot. The campground forms a C as it curves around a tidal creek to its right and a mangrove thicket to its left. A floor of gravel over hard rock makes it challenging to stake your tent. Twenty-two of the forty-seven campsites abut to the tidal creek. A decent cover of buttonwood, palm, gumbo limbo, and sea grape shades the first few campsites, along with some mangrove that grows on the edge of the tidal creek. The shade peters out as the campsites continue to the end of the row.

The second row, with seventeen campsites and little vegetation, shade, or campsite barriers, starts with a bathhouse, then returns toward the marina parking lot. These are the least desirable campsites in the park, though they are somewhat larger than the sites on the other row. Next comes a fence and the entrance to the park ranger's residence. Then the final seven campsites in this row begin. They back up to a mangrove thicket and have adequate shade over them. A second bathhouse lies at the end of this row.

Despite being one of the least appealing of Florida's coastal campgrounds, John Pennekamp stays very busy. It is full virtually every night from December through the winter and beyond into the summer. Even summer weekdays are full. Fall and the threat of hurricanes are the only things that keep campers away. This means make your reservation eleven months in advance if you want to park your rig or pitch your tent at John Pennekamp.

Human and Natural History

Miami newspaperman John D. Pennekamp was a driving force in the establishment of this park, which protects the only living coral reefs off the continental United States. He realized the fragile resources of this undersea wonderland were being harvested and destroyed by private and commercial divers. Now the park's waters are part of the bigger Florida Keys National Marine Sanctuary, which extends from Biscayne Bay to the Dry Tortugas. Different regulations cover different areas, so that this region of marine sanctuary can be used in many ways while simultaneously being protected for the future.

The coral reefs of John Pennekamp are ocean habitats that provide a foundation for many marine plants and animals. These corals are huge, live colonies made up of tiny individuals known as polyps. A limestone skeleton forms from polyp secretions, and new polyps grow on the skeletons. This limestone is the stuff that forms the reefs. Around these reefs are other living corals, without skeletons, and a host of undersea creatures such as the spiny lobster, turtles, and lots of fish.

Another important plant community of the Keys Marine Sanctuary is the seagrass meadows. These seagrasses are one of the few flowering plants that grow entirely under water. Thick stands of seagrass cleanse the water and stabilize the ocean floor while providing food for manatees, turtles, shrimp, and smaller fish, which in turn attract larger fish and birds. These seagrass meadows form a buffer between the coral reefs and the Keys themselves, preventing sediment from settling on and harming the corals.

Mangroves also act as a filter for trapping land debris, and they provide habitat for small fish. Together, these three communities—coral reefs, seagrass meadows, and mangroves—help keep the ocean clean and alive.

What To Do

As a warm-up, head to the park visitor center and check out the thirty-thousand-gallon aquarium. In it a reef environment is re-created. The spiny lobsters and tropical fish are quite a sight. Enjoy the video on the park and environs. Now you are primed for the real thing. All of the equipment and instruction needed to explore the reefs are onsite at John Pennekamp. But if you aren't in the mood to get wet, take a glass-bottomed boat tour. This two-and-a-half-hour trip will give you some spectacular views of life beneath the clear waters.

Snorkeling is easy to learn and doesn't require certification like diving. If you don't feel comfortable renting your gear and hitting the water on your own, join a snorkeling tour and learn with other greenhorns. You can also double your fun by heading to sea on a catamaran and sailing to a good snorkeling location. If snorkeling makes you want to go deeper, certified instructors are available for actual diving lessons. If you already know how to dive, you can get openwater or advanced openwater certification. Anglers enjoy these waters too, getting only their lines wet, fishing for a variety of saltwater species.

Two short nature trails will familiarize you with the flora of the area. The Tamarind Trail explores a tropical hardwood hammock. The Mangrove Trail follows a boardwalk through a shoreline mangrove thicket. Look down from the observation tower over the salt-tolerant trees, or view the mangrove from the water upward by canoe or kayak on a 2.5-mile marked trail through the trees.

Of course, you'll also find Cannon Beach and Far Beach. You may need a few hours of relaxation after exploring America's first undersea park.

What's Nearby

The coral reefs are the primary attraction of Key Largo and environs. But just to the northwest of Key Largo is the vastness of the Everglades National Park. There is a world of nature to explore there. Ten miles south of John Pennekamp is the Florida Keys Wild Bird Rehabilitation Center. Here injured birds are nursed and released into the wild. You can see these birds as they recover. The *African Queen*, the boat made famous by the movie of the same name starring Humphrey Bogart and Katherine Hepburn, is on display nearby.

An onsite park concessionaire has a snack bar and limited supplies. Just as few miles south on US 1 is a full-service grocery store and a discount store. Two recommended eateries are Gus' Grill, which serves Floribbean fare, and Sundowners, which offers steaks and seafood.

Long Key State Recreation Area

You'll have a hard time finding a campground with more crystal-clear sky blue sea around it than at Long Key. Set in the center of the Florida Keys with the Atlantic Ocean on one side and Florida Bay on the other, this state recreation area not only has an oceanside campground, it is also prime site for watersports. The Middle Keys are often called the sport-fishing capital of the world, but the most beautiful water in the state might keep you from focusing on your rod. That exquisite aquamarine water is why boating, canoeing, and studying marine ecology also draw people here. So does looking over the Atlantic Ocean from your campsite.

Cloudy day at the Long Key campground.

Key Information

Long Key State Recreation Area
US 1 Post Office Box 776
Long Key, FL 33001
(305) 664-4815

Sites: 60

Amenities: Picnic table, fire ring, water spigot, electricity

Registration: By phone or at park entrance booth

Facilities: Hot showers, flush toilets, pay phone, soda machine

Fees: $24 per night, $2 electricity

Directions: Long Key State Recreation Area is at mile marker 67.5 on US 1.

Why wouldn't the water be a draw? From the mainland to Key West there is far more ocean than land. The resources of the sea have drawn humans here for thousands of years, creating an interesting history that you can learn about while at Long Key. Nearby are two state-owned islands, Lignumvitae Key and Indian Key, which are sites where this history is preserved.

The Beach/Coast

Though there is a lot of water around, there is less classic beach than you might imagine. In most of the Keys, the tropical forest and mangrove grow right to the water, with minimal sandy transition areas before you get to stunning sea. But don't let that stop you. There are enough sandy spots to lay your body down, just not enough to throw your Frisbee.

The north side of Long Key, which faces Florida Bay, is exposed rocky coral reef leading right to the water. In other areas mangrove forms the transition area between land and sea. The east side of Long Key is known as Long Key Bight. This is a shallow area that forms a bay lined in mangrove with small channels and mangrove islands.

As you move south around Long Key Point, the mangrove gives way to a narrow strip of beach looking out over the Atlantic Ocean. Just a few miles out to sea is the warm Gulf Stream, the current where so many ships travel. The reefs of the Keys lie perilously close to the Gulf Stream, and this has resulted in many shipwrecks offshore. In fact, the salvage business has been an important part of Keys history.

The most popular swimming location is beyond the shaded picnic area. Here rocks line the island, preventing erosion. A small pier has steps that lead right to the water. Farther down is the campground. A narrow beach backed by a small dune runs parallel to the ocean. Swimmers can be found here too. Here and there a stray mangrove grows. This narrow beach extends beyond the campground to the end of the park.

The Campground

This campground affords one of the best views in the state, possibly in the country. Every one of the sixty campsites overlooks the Atlantic Ocean. The water offshore is aquamarine, with darker patches of blue off in the distance. Overhead are shade-rendering Australian pines with an understory of native plants—tropical vegetation that within the United States is found only in the Keys.

Pass the always-locked campground gate and enter the site, which is laid out along one slender paved road. All of the campsites are to your left and beyond the sea. Off to your right are a section of plant growth and US 1. This section of Long Key is narrow, but the Keys are land-poor to start with, so the drone of US 1 is hard to escape anywhere down here. Let it be known that road noise is a drawback. It's the price you pay for the fantastic ocean view.

The campsites are generally more narrow than they are wide, though an average RV can fit into almost any site, especially now that water and electricity are installed at every campsite. Park personnel have worked hard to plant native vegetation between campsites to provide natural privacy barriers and to restore the park to something approaching its original state. Now such tropical trees as seven-year apple, poisonwood, buttonwood, and gumbo limbo adorn the campground.

Between the ocean and each campsite is a small wooden dune barrier that protects the sea oats and shoreline plants. But the unobtrusive barrier leaves open a small path that leads from each campsite to the seaside. Wooden logs have been laid out to delineate exact campsite boundaries. Pitch your tent or park your rig on a floor of sand and pine needles.

The middle of the campground is the most wooded and shaded area. Australian pines form a shady canopy over the campsites and the road. Some of the park's biggest sites are in this area. Farther down, the sites become smaller, but here you have less campground traffic to deal with. Past the last site is a campfire circle and a small auto turnaround area. Three separate bathhouses are evenly spaced along the campground road.

This campground is at its busiest from mid-December to mid-March. It is rare to find a campsite unoccupied during this time. Don't waste your time driving down and taking your chances—make a reservation. The crowds ease up when the snowbirds depart, though you can expect a full house on summer holidays. Even with the recent installation of water and electricity at every campsite, the tent to RV ratio has remained about fifty-fifty, with a heavier mix of RVs in the winter.

Human and Natural History

Calusa Indians occupied the Keys until the arrival of Europeans. The Spanish lost the islands to the English. The islands eventually came under the American flag. As international involvement grew in the New World, so did shipping. The use of the Gulf Stream inevitably led to shipwrecks, and Key West became an important wreck-salvaging center.

Then, one Jacob Housman decided to establish his own wrecking center on Indian Key, a few miles northeast of Long Key. The Gulf Stream was very close to the reefs there, so he was in proximity to many wrecks. The plan worked, and it made Housman wealthy and his competition in Key West angry, especially after he convinced the state to form Dade County with Indian Key as county seat. The Key Westers of Monroe County took him to court and finally drove him out of business.

A Dr. Henry Perrine came to Indian Key during the Second Seminole War, and under government funding he tried to develop uses for the tropical plants of the area. But he was killed by the Indians.

The area remained remote until Henry Flagler extended the Florida East Coast Railroad to Key West. With that, Long Key entered its golden age. With author Zane Grey at the helm, the Long Key Fishing Club established a plush fishing resort there. Famous anglers from around the world fished these waters and established a policy of protecting many of the gamefish they sought. In 1935 a hurricane wiped out the railroad and fishing club, as well as a coconut plantation that was on the site of Long Key Recreation Area. Later, US 1 was built on fill and pilings from the old railroad, establishing auto access from the mainland to the Keys and what we see today.

Nearby Lignumvitae Key is the site of the homesite of William J. Matheson, who bought the island in 1919. This remote island has fascinating tropical hammock forest seen only in the Keys.

What To Do

Being an island surrounded by ocean, Long Key is geared toward water-oriented activities. You can simply step forth from your campsite and take a dip in the beautiful waters of the Atlantic. Swimming and snorkeling are also delightful in these clear waters. You'll also find fishermen wading beyond the campsites trying to nail bonefish. You can fish from a canoe in the Atlantic or in Florida Bay, or head south just a short way on US 1 and angle from the old bridge between Long Key and Conch Key. Hogfish, grouper, and snapper are tasty treats that may end up on your hook. There are bait and tackle shops all over the Keys.

If you want to plunk down some money, you can rent a boat or take a charter, but here is an alternative. Consider taking what I call a "head" boat. This is one of those group charters that charges by the "head." You won't get the personalized pampering of a private charter, but you may just catch some fish.

If you don't fish but still want to get out on the fantastic water, take a tour boat out to Lignumvitae and Indian Key. A ranger will show you around the historic islands and help you explore the natural and cultural history of these places. I recommend Robbie Marina, which is located a few miles north of Long Key. The marina phone number is (305) 664-9814.

Back at Long Key, trail lovers can walk the Golden Orb Trail, which pierces the mangrove to the beach then comes back again. The Layton Trail across US 1 enters a dark tropical hammock and gives hikers the opportunity to identify all the unusual fauna of Long Key. Canoers can paddle the Long Key Lakes in the safety of

Long Key Bight. Bicyclers can pedal park roads out to US 1 and follow a paved path that leads in both directions back to the civilized world.

What's Nearby

North of you is Islamorada, "the Purple Isles." This is where Lignumvitae Key and Indian Key are located. South of you is Marathon. Marathon is the heart of the Keys and the nearest source of a full-service grocery store and other major supply shops. There is a convenience store just north of the park.

Another beach area is Annes Beach, about ten miles north of the park along US 1. The beach is wider than the beach at Long Key, but not by much.

There are two good restaurants just around the corner from the park. Little Italy serves Italian and American cuisine, along with some fine seafood. Prices are very reasonable. Just south of the park is the Tea Colony Inn. It also has American cuisine and fresh seafood at prices that won't break the bank.

Bahia Honda State Park

It's the beaches. The beaches are the number-one attraction at Bahia Honda State Park. For all that coastline they have, there are surprisingly few beaches in the Keys, so any beach is better than no beach. But Bahia Honda is blessed not only with three beaches but what many call the best beaches in south Florida. In fact, in 1992 Sandspur Beach was voted the best beach in the entire United States.

The beaches may be one drawing card, but there are other attractions. The three park campgrounds all offer a different view of this 524-acre park, of which 366 acres is classified as nonsubmergible land. But the orientation here is, surprisingly, not entirely toward the water. This translucent aquamarine sea, broken

A day at Sandspur Beach.

Key Information

Bahia Honda State Park
36850 Overseas Highway
Big Pine Key, FL 33043
(305) 872-2353

Sites: 66 water and electric, 16 water only

Amenities: Picnic table, grill, water spigot

Registration: By phone or at park entrance booth

Facilities: Hot showers, flush toilets, pay phone

Fees: $24 per night, $2 waterfront site, $2 electricity

Directions: Bahia Honda State Park is on your left at mile marker 36.5 on us 1.

up by darker patches of seagrass, offers fishing, boating, snorkeling, kayaking, and every other mode of movement over water, including parasailing!

Attractiveness draws a crowd. Bahia Honda is positively hopping. Campers make reservations. And when you arrive, relax, take your time, and enjoy the park. Make sure to schedule a day to visit Key West and a day to enjoy the fantastic sport fishing of the Lower Keys.

The Beach/Coast

Tropical flora, stunningly colorful and clear water, and a little sand combine to make some great beach at Bahia Honda. Just below the Buttonwood Camping Area and the marina is Calusa Beach. Picnic shelters and palm trees border the roped-off swim area. The calm waters are ideal for young children.

On the south side of the old railroad bridge is the Atlantic Ocean and a continuous stretch of scenic shoreline. The picnic area has wooden walkways leading to the beach. Next up the coast is Loggerhead Beach. Four walkways lead from old US 1 down to the sand. This beach is continuous and enters a small cove broken up by a tidal creek flowing in and out of a lagoon in the key's interior. Past the cove is a stretch of exposed Key Largo limestone, the foundation of the island. Boardwalks connect the limestone to the campsites of the Sandspur Camping Area.

Then you arrive at the park's best beach, Sandspur. Two picnic shelters flank a central bathhouse. The beach is wide, especially by Keys standards. The waters are often calm and nearly always clear. Boaters are seen out on the horizon. Nearby, beach goers are engaged in a variety of pursuits, including doing absolutely nothing. Sandspur Beach extends to the channel between Bahia Honda and Ohio Key. This channel is lined with mangrove, as is the north side of Bahia Honda, though there are rocky areas of exposed limestone. Then you come to the dredged deep inlet by the park cabins and Bay Side Camping Area and finally to US 1.

The Campground

The three camping areas at Bahia Honda each exude a different ambiance. The Buttonwood Camping Area is just south of US 1. This is the sole campground RVers can use. The forty-eight sites, all with water and electricity, are divided along three rows. The vegetation, featuring palms and sea grape, is dense between the campsites but is low-slung and offers little shade overhead. The first row of campsites, which abuts a mangrove stand, has the most vegetation. Along this row is a fully equipped bathhouse.

The second row is more open and has campsites on both sides. It is the least appealing in the Buttonwood area. The third row runs parallel to the ocean and ends in a little turnaround. The campsites have the least growth around them but make up for it with the ocean view and breezes. Adjacent to this row there are some slips for campers' boats. But the campsites also face out to the noisy highway.

Pass under the low clearance of US 1 and come to the Bay Side Camping Area. It has eight sites in a row along an old dredged inlet. These sites, with water only, are for tents, vans, and pop-ups that can go below the six-foot-eight-inch clearance of US 1. Depending on the campsite the tropical flora provides some shade, but you should get some decent ocean breezes. A new bathhouse has been constructed to serve these campers. This area has very little traffic, but the proximity to US 1 is a drawback.

Set apart from the others is the Sandspur Camping Area. The twenty-four campsites here are stretched along a road leading through an oceanside tropical hammock. The woods there are dense with gumbo limbo and buttonwood. The campsites are literally cut out of the forest. Breezes are nil, and the sites may be buggy at times.

The first eight sites have water only and are away from the ocean in the darkest woods. Stay here if you are a shade lover. Come to the fully equipped bathhouse and a boardwalk leading to the ocean. Then you'll find the next sixteen campsites, all with water and electricity. Eleven are oceanside yet have wooden dune barriers to create a single path leading to the shore to protect the shoreline vegetation. These campsites are the best in the park. You get a combination of shade and ocean access and maybe even some breezes. The thick hammock dulls the sounds of US 1.

This campground is busy nearly all the time. From December through May the campground is full every night. A few summer weeknights see some vacancies. Fall is the least busy time, but don't take chances. Make your reservations as far in advance as possible. The park will take reservations up to eleven months ahead of your visit.

Human and Natural History

Just a few miles southwest of Bahia Honda is Big Pine Key, primary habitat for one of the rarest, most threatened, and cutest animal species in the United States—the Key deer. These small deer, a subspecies of the Virginia white-tailed deer, stand only two to three feet high at the shoulder. Back in the 1940s their very existence was in peril. Less than forty individuals were known to exist. But in 1957 the National Key Deer Refuge was established, and the population has stabilized at around three hundred animals. Most are on Big Pine Key and No Name Key, but they range from the Johnson Keys in the east to the Sugarloaf Keys in the west.

It is believed that the deer migrated to the area during the last ice age, when the Keys were a continuous land bridge. As the ice melted the sea rose, forming the Keys and limiting the range of the deer. Indians, Spaniards, and wreck salvagers used the deer as a food source. Uncontrolled hunting and loss of habitat brought the deer to the brink of extinction before the establishment of the refuge. You can visit the National Key Deer Refuge on Big Pine Key. It is located just off US 1 on Key Deer Boulevard. The refuge is open from sunrise to sunset.

Now the deer can feed on the mangrove, palm berries, and other vegetation. Also critical to their existence is fresh water. Big Pine Key is generally higher than other Keys, resulting in an upwelling of fresh water beneath the land. Especially important is the Blue Hole, an old freshwater quarry.

Nowadays the biggest threat to the Key deer's survival is the traffic of US 1. Some deer will be hit by cars—that's inevitable. But when you're driving on Big Pine Key, please slow down and keep your eyes peeled. Another problem for the deer is human contact. Feeding these rare deer attracts them to roads, where they may be poached or struck by vehicles. They're beautiful, but don't do it. Help nurture and preserve these rare jewels of the Keys.

What To Do

With three beaches in the park, your main task is to find the one you like. There are miles of sand and even more miles of water. Relaxation and escape from the rat race seem to be the main adult diversion. Building sand castles works for kids. Other folks will be fishing. Snorkeling is rewarding in the clear water. Sea kayaks are another popular way to get on the ocean. If you want to get above the water, take a parasailing ride. The park concessionaire rents them along with just about everything else you night need at Bahia Honda: pontoon boats, fishing boats, one- and two-person kayaks, fishing rods, and bicycles.

It would be a shame to come to the Keys and not spend a day enjoying some fantastic sport fishing. If you agree, then Captain Hunter Donaldson of Big Pine Key is the man for you. Step aboard his boat, known as *Genuine Draft*, and head out into the water for a day of fishing that will surely inspire tales of big and plentiful fish. And you won't even have to exaggerate. Hunter runs a first-class operation that I have often enjoyed on my trips to the Keys. I highly recommend his friendly service.

In the summer you can fish for dolphin, wahoo, tuna, and billfish. In the winter Hunter will steer you toward king mackerel, sailfish, and smaller dolphin. And don't forget the year-round snapper and grouper fishery. He'll also help you achieve the backcountry grand slam—bonefish, permit, and tarpon. May and June are the trophy tarpon-fishing months. Hunter's phone number is (305) 872-9722.

What's Nearby

Many campers use Bahia Honda as a base to explore famed Key West, a place steeped in history, from the days of the Spaniards to Fort Zachary Taylor and from wreck salvagers to Ernest

Hemingway. Take the Conch Train and tour Old Town and Duval Street. Climb the Key West Lighthouse and enjoy the view. The Key West Shipwreck Historeum will inform you about the boats that foundered in the shifting shoals of the southernmost United States.

For supplies, there is a small store and snack bar at Bahia Honda, but the nearest full-service grocery and supply stores are six miles south on Big Pine Key. If you want some good food head a few miles north to Marathon and try the 7 Mile Grill. It's open for breakfast, lunch, and dinner and serves a mean fish sandwich. Also in Marathon is Panchos, where you'll find seafood, steaks, and Mexican food at reasonable rates.